MARIAH CAREY

Biography

The Life Story of the Christmas Queen

Rafael Sanchez

Copyright © 2023
All rights reserved

The content of this book may not be reproduced, duplicated, or transmitted without the author's or publisher's express written permission. Under no circumstances will the publisher or author be held liable or legally responsible for any damages, reparation, or monetary loss caused by the information contained in this book, whether directly or indirectly.

Legal Notice:
This publication is copyrighted. It is strictly for personal use only. You may not change, distribute, sell, use, quote, or paraphrase any part of this book without the author's or publisher's permission.

Disclaimer Notice:
Please keep in mind that the information in this document is only for educational and entertainment purposes. Every effort has been made to present accurate, up-to-date, reliable, and comprehensive information. There are no express or implied warranties. Readers understand that the author is not providing legal, financial, medical, or professional advice. This book's content was compiled from a variety of sources. Please seek the advice of a licensed professional before attempting any of the techniques described in this book. By reading this document, the reader agrees that the author is not liable for any direct or indirect losses incurred as a result of using the information contained within this document, including, but not limited to, errors, omissions, or inaccuracies.

TABLE OF CONTENTS

Part I: Wayward Child

An Intention

Existence

Close My Eyes

There Can be Miracles

When Christmas Comes

The Father and the Sun

Coloring Outside the Lines

Hodel

Light of My Life

Dandelion Tea

Detangled and Swept Away

A Girl's Best Friend

Part II: Sing. Sing.

A Prelude to Sing Sing

Alone in Love

Cherchez La Femme

Princess. Prisoner.

A Family

My Big Fat Sony Wedding

Thanksgiving is Cancelled!

The Man From Kalamazoo

The Last Show at Sing Sing

Part III: All That Glitters

Firecracker

Calamity and Dog Hair

Snow globe of joy

PART I: WAYWARD CHILD

An Intention

My objective was to keep her safe, yet I may only have succeeded in keeping her imprisoned.

She's been locked away inside of me for many years, always alone, hidden in plain sight in front of crowds. There's a lot of her in my early work: she's commonly found peering out windows, dwarfed by a large frame, barefoot, staring at an empty rope swing swaying from a lone tree against a purple evening sky. Alternatively, she could be two storeys up in a brownstone, watching the local kids dance on the pavement below. She's shown up in an OshKosh overalls school auditorium, cradling a ball on the sidelines, waiting and longing to be chosen. On a roller coaster or speeding by on skates with her hands in the air, she is occasionally captured in a rare moment of delight. But she always stays as a vague longing just behind my eyes. She's been terrified and alone for so long, yet she's never lost her light in the darkness. Her yearning has been heard over the airwaves and seen on screens, and she has made herself known through my music. Millions of people have heard of her but have never met her.

She is Mariah, and here is most of her narrative as she saw it.

My first memories are of violent incidents. As a result, I've always carried a huge blanket with me to cover up large chunks of my upbringing. It's been a strain. But I can't take the weight of that blanket or the silence of the tiny girl suffocating beneath it any longer. I'm a mature woman now, with my own little child and boy. I've seen, I've been afraid, I've been scarred, and I've lived. I've used my music and voice to encourage people while also emancipating myself as an adult. I give this book in part to finally free the fearful little girl inside of me. It's time to give her a voice, to let her tell her story the way she saw it.

Though you can't argue with someone's lived experience, details in this book will undoubtedly differ from the narratives of my family, friends, and numerous people who think they know me. I've been living in that conflict for far too long, and I'm sick of it. In an attempt to protect others, I put my palm over that small girl's mouth. Even "those others" who never attempted to shield me. Despite my best efforts to "be above it all," I was dragged, sued, and ripped off. I only ended up hurting her more, and it nearly killed me.

This book is a testament to the perseverance of silent young girls and boys around the world in insisting that we believe them. To pay tribute to their experiences and relate their stories. To liberate them.

Existence

There was a period in my youth when I didn't believe I deserved to be alive. I was too young to consider suicide, but I was old enough to realize I hadn't started living or found my place in the world. Nobody in my environment looked like me or mirrored how I felt on the inside.

My mother, Patricia, had whiter skin and straighter hair, and my father, Alfred Roy, had darker skin and kinkier hair, and neither had faces like mine. I regarded them both as victims of a series of tragic circumstances, plagued with sorrow. Alison, my sister, and Morgan, my brother, were both older and darker, and not simply in terms of skin colour, though they were slightly browner. They each seemed to have a similar energy that seemed to block light. They had a worldview that left little room for whimsy and fantasy, which was my natural nature. We were related by blood, but I felt like an outsider among them, an intruder in my own family.

I was always terrified as a child, and music was my escape. My home was weighed down by yelling and confusion. It helped to calm me down to sing in a whispery tone. I discovered a peaceful, gentle, light area within my voice-a vibration within me that provided me with exquisite relief. My hushed singing was my own lullaby to myself.

But singing allowed me to connect with my mother, a Juilliard-trained opera singer. The repeating of the scales felt like a chant to my frightened little mind as I listened to her doing vocal exercises at home. Her voice soared and fell, up and down, up and up, and up-and something inside me rose with it. (I'd also sing along to Minnie Riperton's wonderful, angelic, soulful "Lovin' You" and follow her voice up into the clouds.) To my mother's delight, I would sing tiny tunes around the home. And she was always encouraging. She kept faltering on this one part while practising an aria from the opera Rigoletto. I returned her song in flawless Italian. I was about three years old. She glanced at me, astonished, and I knew she saw me at that instant. To her, I was more than just a little girl. Mariah was my name. A performer of music.

Before I could talk, my father taught me to whistle. Even back then, I had a raspy speaking voice that I appreciated since it set me apart from most other kids my age. My singing voice, on the other hand, was rich and powerful. I was strolling down the street with my friend Maureen, who had porcelain-like complexion, soft brown hair, and a charming face like Dorothy from The Wizard of Oz, when I was around eight years old. She was one of the neighbourhood's few small white girls who was allowed to play with me. I started singing something as we walked. She came to a halt on the sidewalk, locked in place. She stood quite still and listened for a moment. Finally, she turned to me and remarked, clearly and steadily, "When you sing, it sounds like you're accompanied by instruments." Your voice is surrounded by music." She stated it as if it were a pronouncement, nearly a prayer.

They say God talks through individuals, and I'll be eternally grateful to my little girlfriend for speaking into my heart that day. She recognized something wonderful in me and put words to it, and I trusted her. My voice, I thought, was formed of instruments-piano, strings, and flutes. I thought my voice could be a melody. All I wanted was for someone to notice and listen to me.

I observed how my voice could make people feel wonderful on the inside, how it could be miraculous and transformational. That meant not only was I not unworthy or insignificant as a person, but I was also valuable. The feeling was something valuable that I could share with others. It was the sensation I would seek for the rest of my life. It provided me with a cause to exist.

Close My Eyes

It took twelve cops to separate my brother and father. The large bodies of men smashed into the living room, entwined like a spinning hurricane. In an instant, I lost sight of familiar things: no windows, no floor, no furniture, and no light. All I could see was a tangle of limbs knotted together and tearing away, and heavy, polished black shoes scuffling and stomping. There were brief flashes of sparkling objects such as buttons, badges, and firearms. At least a dozen pistol handles sat on wide black belts across broad hips, stiff and jutting out of dull leather holsters, a few cradled in hands and thumbs. The noises of cursing, moaning, and wailing filled the air. The entire home appeared to be trembling. And somewhere in the eye of this tempest, the two most important male characters in my life were annihilating each other.

My brother's rage had always struck me as fierce, destructive, and unexpected. I'm not sure if it was a single incident or a chronic disease that caused him to be so explosive, but that was all I had ever known.

I was a tiny girl with little recollections of a big brother who looked out for me. More often than not, I felt compelled to defend myself against him, and on occasion, I found myself defending my mother against him as well.

However, our disagreement with our father had escalated more swiftly than usual. In what seemed like an instant, a shouting brawl turned into a tornado of fists, pounding through the room, knocking things over, and wreaking mayhem. My father and brother's fury was so intense at the time that no one could have stopped it. Nobody would have ventured to.

I had evolved the instincts to detect impending violence by the time I was a child. As if I could smell rain, I could detect when adult yelling reached a particular pitch and velocity, indicating that I should take cover. It was not uncommon for holes to be punched in walls or for other objects to fly when my brother was present. I never knew how or why the fights started, but I did know when tension turned into an argument and when an argument turned into a physical fight. And I had a feeling this one was going to be big.

My Nana Reese was there, which was unusual because she and my father's family, who resided in Harlem, were rarely at our house. We lived in Melville, a predominantly white, affluent-neighbouring town in Suffolk County on Long Island, New York, though I moved thirteen times as a child. Thirteen times to pack up and leave, to try to find somewhere else-a better, safer place. Thirteen new beginnings, thirteen new streets, and thirteen new homes full of people who will judge you and wonder where or who your father is. Thirteen times to be called unfit and dismissed, to be sent to the sidelines.

My father was raised by Pastor Nana Reese, the Reverend Roscoe Reese, and their African Methodist Pentecostal Church. Roy was Nana Reese's sister and Addie's only son. My father never lived with his father, and there was always a powerful gap between them, a mystery that always contained sadness. These individuals, who lived in Harlem, were his people. They had migrated up from Alabama, sections of North Carolina, and other southern states, carrying with them old, African, and magical traditions, traumas, and gifts.

Nana Reese and I met just as all hell was about to break out. All other sounds were drowned out by the thunder of obscenities, fists, and feet, so I didn't hear when the officers stormed in.

I couldn't tell if they had come to save or murder us. It was the 1970s on Long Island, and two Black males were fighting-the arrival of the police virtually never indicated that help had arrived. On the contrary, their presence frequently compounded and escalated existing terror and violence. That hasn't changed, but this is the first time I've encountered this fact. I had no experience; I had no advantage of any kind. Nana Reese's daughter, my cousin LaVinia, used to say, "You kids had all the burdens of being Black but none of the benefits." It took me a long time to grasp the significance of her observation.

Of course, this was hardly my father and brother's first brawl-their relationship had been a battleground for as long as I could remember. It was, however, the first time the army had been brought in. It was also the first time I witnessed a member of my family being brutally murdered in front of my eyes. Or that I might perish as well. I was just four years old.

My mother and father lived in Brooklyn Heights together until their marriage became miserable. Though the area had seen a stream of bohemians enter as early as 1910, and the 1950s saw a wave of urban activists-liberal folks with money who despised the suburbs-it was still a relatively diversified mix of primarily working- and middle-class families in the 1970s. It was ungentrified and pre-yuppie. If there was a friendly neighbourhood for a young mixed-race family at the time, Brooklyn Heights was probably the closest thing to it.

Throughout my childhood, I lived in a variety of remote locations, usually on Long Island, and felt like a castaway on this island-off-the-island of Manhattan. My parents both worked extremely hard to ensure that we could live in places where we might see that elusive "better life" and feel "safe." However, conventional thinking holds that "better" and "safe" are associated with white.

We were not a typical family. Was it better to live in a neighbourhood where my white mother would frequently come alone through the front door first, ahead of my Black father and her mixed-race children, for their safety? What effect does this have on the mind of a man who is supposed to be the head of the household? How can such a father keep his family safe, and what message does such humiliation send to his Black son?

Everyone was alive once the police officers separated my father and brother, despite the fact that there was still a lot of yelling. The truly scary phase of the storm had passed; the thunder had died away. I was crying and trembling in Nana Reese's arms the next thing I knew. She'd snatched me up like a sack of laundry and placed me next to her on "the rocking couch," a cheap, fragile construction the colour of dirt, rust, and olive, flecked with mustard. That couch, I believe, established the seed of my ultimate preference for Chanel. We called it the "rocking couch" since it was missing a leg and, well, rocked as you shifted your weight back and forth. This was a brave endeavour to find humour in the midst of shattered things, a skill I shared with my brother and sister. On that awful sofa, in the midst of the violence and trauma, a wonderful comfort came to me.

Nana Reese gripped me tightly until my little body stopped shivering and my breathing returned to normal. I returned to the room, to my body, after being disoriented. She pushed my face up toward the light, making sure my gaze was fixed on hers. She forcefully placed her delicate hand on my thigh. Her touch instantly calmed any aftershocks that were still running through me. Her eyes were not those of a great-aunt, a mother, or a doctor. Instead, it was as if she had peered directly into my soul. We were not a terrified small girl and a comforting elder at that moment, but two souls, timeless and equal.

"Don't be afraid of all the trouble you see," she said. All of your dreams and aspirations will come true. Always keep that in mind."

A warm and loving energy flowed from her hand to my leg, slowly coursing through my body in waves and rising up and out the top of my head as she spoke. A passage had been washed clear through the devastation; I knew there was light. And I knew that light was mine and would remain forever. I couldn't recall any dreams prior to that point. I, too, had little memories. I certainly hadn't heard a song or had a vision yet.

I didn't see my Nana Reese much after my parents divorced when I was four years old. My mother's and father's families remained at odds, and because I lived with my mother, I was mostly cut off from Nana's life of healing and holy rolling in Harlem. I later learned that Nana Reese was referred to as a "prophetess." I also discovered that she was not the only healer in my family. Aside from that, I believe that day reawakened a profound faith in me.

On a soul level, I realised that no matter what occurred to me or around me, there was something inside me that I could always draw on. I had something to help me get through any storm.

There Can be Miracles

My mother relocated my brother and me into a little, unassuming house in Northport, Long Island, when we were six years old. It perched miserably atop a long, twisting concrete stairwell.

The uninteresting edifice comprised a few tiny rooms on either side of a steep, rickety staircase that led up to even smaller rooms. Morgan was often left to babysit me because my mother was often busy or out late at night. He lacked the necessary skills to care for a young girl. He would abandon me and go wild with his adolescent mates. I was alone one night and was watching a 20/20 show on stolen children-completely unsuitable for a six-year-old. And just then, several kids in the area decided to throw rocks through the window. "Mariah, we're gonna get you!" their voices pierced the black night. I was afraid of the news, the kids, the night, the house, and my complete isolation.

I wished for my brother's affection. His powerful energy astonished me, but it also terrified me. This small house couldn't possibly support all of our anguish and dread, especially my brother's. It was a rough period. My mother was sad, and my brother-well, let's just say he was more than an angry teen, especially in high school. By middle school, he'd gone from fury to full-fledged rage. My younger brother was brimming with creative and physical potential as an adolescent. However, he had previously been tormented and beaten up for having a disability and being a mixed-race child. His apparent racial difference constantly separated him from the white boys on Long Island and made him a target. When regular meanness is mixed with racism, it takes on a special cruelty, one that is frequently sanctioned by (and learnt from) adults. My brother most certainly received some abuse from the Black youngsters as well. I'm sure his remoteness from their observable Blackness, the kind that gets you roughed up by cops for no reason, instilled hatred in them that manifested itself in physical blows and name-calling.

Early on, my brother was damaged, and the only weapon he had to defend himself was destruction. He would fight everything, including his demons and others, notably our father. His bond with our father did not help him rebuild; instead, it dragged him deeper into his inner anguish. A broken man can't mend his broken son. My brother had been smashed into bits and dispersed to the wind, and our father's antiquated weapons of military discipline were insufficient to help him gather himself and prepare for manhood. My brother's constant and crushing suffering stemmed from our father's misunderstanding and emotional remoteness, which resulted in his total fury.

For the majority of my youth, I was caught between my brother's rage and my mother's despondent search. Both rage and despondency are extremely harmful, but I believe one moves within and the other outward. When they collide, the results might be disastrous. By the time I was in kindergarten, disaster had become commonplace to me. Mini eruptions erupted between my mother and brother on a daily basis when we lived in Northport. I trained myself to remain still and wait for the eruptions to pass. I mostly tuned out the words and reasons for their fights-the "why" was big-people territory. Their disputes were a jumble of heated voices at high volume, punctuated by merciless profanity, to me.

One night, however, I understood exactly what was causing the argument: my brother wanted to use my mother's car, and she wouldn't let him. They'd certainly had hundreds of arguments over the automobile, but this night felt different. I was paying close attention. Normally, their fights would begin how I imagined normal fights between most teenagers and their parents would, but not this time. It started out as a blow-up and quickly escalated into violent curses being hurled across the room. Hurtful remarks ricocheted off the walls like bullets, gathering strength with each subsequent round. The yelling shot from room to room, up and down the stairs, and the entire home turned into a battlefield. There was nowhere to hide. As my mother and brother stood face to face, barely inches of electrified wrath separated them, I felt the air thicken. I was scared. My entire body tensed. I locked my gaze on the gap between them and yelled out, "Stop it! Stop it!" through my tears over and over. I was hoping that my sobbing might enter that place and temporarily disable them.

There was a loud, sharp noise, like a gunshot. My brother had shoved my mother so hard that she smacked into the wall, generating a loud shattering sound. I noticed her frame stiffen; she appeared frozen against the wall, stuck up like a painting, her feet lifted several inches off the ground. She was completely limp, as if her bones had melted, and folded into the floor the next thing I knew. It was only a fraction of a second. It felt like an eternity. My eyes remained stuck in place, but now I was staring at my mother, who was crumpled in a heap on the floor. My brother stomped out, slammed the door, and sped away in her car, rocking the house one more time.

I stood there in the strange silence for a moment. I could hear my own breathing but couldn't tell if my mother was still alive. A frightening clarity struck me just as a soft part of my childhood faded away. I drew myself together without moving my gaze away from my motionless mother. When I picked up the receiver of our one phone, I felt it was heavy and cold on my small ear. My small fingers pressed the square buttons in a familiar pattern. It was the phone number of one of my mother's acquaintances, whose home she would occasionally visit to socialise. Hers was one of the few numbers I remembered having just been six years old.

Clearing my throat to be heard above the static hum of the phone, I tried to tell her quietly, "My brother really hurt my mother, and I'm home alone." Please come and assist." I'm not sure what she said. I hung up the phone, my gaze still riveted on my mother's body. I fell into a trance-like state.

I'm not sure how long I stood there, but I snapped out of it when I heard a loud banging on the door. I dashed inside to unlock it for my mother's friend, and numerous cops rushed in. I couldn't understand a word they were saying, but I watched as they rushed over to where my mother was lying. She was gone before I realised it. The spell of amazement broke the minute I discovered she was alive, and a flood of terror and worry washed over me-the growing understanding of what had actually occurred, what had almost happened, and what uncertain future lay ahead. I rolled my small body into a ball, clutched myself firmly, and began to cry quietly. As my mother regained consciousness, I could hear the faint sound of her voice. Then I heard a clear voice echoing just above my head. It was a man's voice, and I'll never forget it.

Looking down at me but speaking to another cop beside him, one of the cops stated, "If this kid makes it, it'll be a miracle." That night, I transformed from a child to a marvel.

<u>When Christmas Comes</u>

For the day, my mother added a leaf to her modest wooden table, making it almost family-sized. With a few basic decorations, the table, along with a Charlie Brown-esque tree, became the joyous highlight of an otherwise unfurnished living room in the run-down house where the two of us resided. Regardless of our circumstances, my mother wished for us to have a "wonderful life."

The days running up to Christmas were a special occasion. My mother kept an Advent calendar every year. Each day, we would open a new flap. She'd give me the chocolates buried inside after I read the piece of a story or poem printed there. The warm spicy aroma of the mulled wine she made disguised the dampness of the house. I was fully aware that we didn't have much money, so while I never expected to receive any lavish gifts or popular goods, I appreciated that we'd make an attempt to get into the spirit and do what we could to create an atmosphere of joy and jubilation. We would clean up, decorate, and, of course, sing. Christmas carols sung in my mother's operatic voice gave our cramped daily lives a sense of spaciousness.

Mother wasn't much of a chef, but she tried-we both tried-for Christmas dinner. We attempted to put all of the pain and drama that had infiltrated the rest of our life on hold in order to enjoy a pleasant Christmas supper. Is that too much to ask? I don't think so. In a house full of disappointment and misery, I was a child yearning for a childhood.

My sister and brother would seldom correspond throughout the year, let alone come to see where my mother and I lived. Christmas was one of the few times when we were all gathered under one decrepit roof. We'd sit around the table, eyes avoiding eyes, frequently unable to speak, blocked up by all the things none of us could express. I was still very young, and I hadn't acquired enough of a past to be broken by it. My siblings and my mother didn't interact for the majority of the year, so my brother and sister would arrive at Christmas dinner loaded with hurt and resentment, yearning for attention. They would all inevitably explode in a flood of verbal abuse at some point. I'd sit in the middle of the turmoil, crying and hoping: that they'd stop screaming, wanting my mother to stop them from cursing. I wished I could be somewhere secure and joyous-anywhere that felt like Christmas.

My sister and brother couldn't bear one other, but their deep anger toward me was a continual, quiet threat seething just beneath the surface. I was the third and youngest kid, and by the time I was three, my parents had divorced. I was what they called a golden child, with lighter hair, skin, and energy. I was living with our mother, and they were separated from one other and from us. They existed in a new type of anguish, absorbing whatever hatred under-loved, unhappy, mixed-race children experience in any community, Black or white. I assumed they thought I was passing. There I was, with my blondish hair, living in a safe white neighbourhood with our white mother. Their animosity at me was maybe the only thing they had in common; they seemed to be connected by it. I understood why they were angry and cruel toward me, but I couldn't understand why they had to ruin Christmas every year.

But my wish was stronger than their agony. I wished enthusiastically. I set about making my own magical, cheerful Christmas wonderland. I concentrated on all my mother had worked so hard to produce; all I needed was a shower of glitter and a full church choir to back me up. Santa Claus, reindeer, snowmen, and all the bells and whistles a small girl's thoughts could hold filled my fantasy Christmas. And I adored looking at a precious baby Jesus and feeling the great joy that the true spirit of the season gives.

My family did not ruin every Christmas.

When I was younger, my mother was culturally liberal and had a varied set of friends. I recall having a buddy, let's call her Ashley, whose mother was lesbian (Ashley had no idea). My mother was straightforward: "Ashley's mom is gay, and she lives with her partner." It's not a huge deal. And it certainly wasn't. Burt and Myron, my guncles (gay uncles), were two of my favourite individuals. They were fantastic, as was their home. It wasn't a lavish affair, but their home was a pleasant midsized brick house set back on a lovely plot of forested land. In the backyard, wild raspberries grew, and they had a golden Labrador named Sparkle. My mother and I would house-sit for them while they went. The cleanliness and comfort delighted me.

Burt was a schoolteacher and photographer, and Myron, as he put it, was a "stay-at-home wife." Myron was a vision in the making. He had a neatly coiffed beard and his hair was constantly blown out in cascading layers that he finished with a dazzling frosting spray. He was always tanned and sashayed around the home in multicoloured silk caftans. Burt would take me out in their yard to snap shots of me (I loved flaunting myself in front of a camera), and he encouraged my dramatic stances. He fully encouraged and appreciated my penchant for extravagance.

I vividly recall one Christmas photo shoot we organised. I was dressed in a green dress with flowers, and I had decent-looking bangs as a special Christmas miracle. I feigned to put an ornament on the tree while looking back over my shoulder, and Burt shot the photo: fashion-feature festive.

Burt and Myron's nice, comfortable little home was especially enjoyable at Christmastime. They put so much thought and personality into getting ready for the season. The house would be immaculately clean, with carefully placed decorations and a roaring fire in the fireplace. They constantly had little delicious morsels to snack on and served sophisticated drinks like brandy Alexanders; the place smelt like a new oven with something roasting inside. I remember being detained at their house during a holiday ice storm that I hoped would never stop. Burt and Myron offered me my first taste of what it was like to have a cosy Christmas. They exemplified a cosy living in general.

My guncles encouraged my inner showgirl. They would give full attention to me whenever I wanted to put on my own little production (which was frequently). They never tried to restrain my wild imagination. "All I Want for Christmas Is You" was inspired by my little girl's spirit and those early fantasies of family and friendship. Consider how it begins: ding, ding, ding, ding, ding, ding, ding, ding, ding, ding, ding, ding, ding, ding, ding, ding... the delicate chimes are reminiscent of those little wooden toy pianos, such as the one Schroeder had on Peanuts.

I did, in fact, pound out the majority of the tune on a cheap tiny

Casio piano. But it's the emotion I intended the song to convey. It has a sweetness, clarity, and purity about it. It was not inspired by Christianity, yet I have sung and written from a soulful and spiritual standpoint. Instead, this song originated from a childlike place; at twenty-two years old, I wasn't that far from being a child when I composed it. I took a risk by recording a complete Christmas CD. Back then, there were no Christmas videos on MTV. It was nearly unheard of for anyone, let alone a young vocalist so early in her career, to create and record an original Christmas song that became a legitimate blockbuster hit.

Though I was accessing my childhood's private dream world in the song, I wasn't in the best of moods when I wrote it. My life had changed so suddenly, and yet I still felt adrift, exploring the wide frontiers between childhood and adulthood. My relationship with Tommy Mottola, who would later become my first husband (and so much more), was already strange, and we hadn't even married yet. But, to his credit as the CEO of my record label, he urged me to record Merry Christmas.

I was feeling nostalgic as well. I've always been painfully sentimental, and Christmas represents that sentimentality for me. I wanted to write a Christmas song that would make me happy and make me feel like a cherished, carefree young girl. I also wanted to deliver it in the style of the greats I grew up idolising, Nat King Cole and the Jackson Five, who had their own Christmas standards. I wanted to sing it in a way that would catch and crystallise everyone's excitement. Yes, I was aiming for vintage Christmas joy. I also believe that somewhere deep down, I realised it was too late to bring my brother and sister peace and my mother's great life to an end, but I could give the world a Christmas classic instead.

The Father and the Sun

My father was like a sunflower to me-tall, haughty, and stoic, but also bright, strong, gorgeous, and self-assured. He worked tirelessly to get up and out of the tough ground in which he was rooted. He was resolved to overcome the limits that his parents, siblings, and generation had encountered. He was the only child of his parents, Robert and Addie. Addie's third-grade schooling humiliated him. Because Addie was strict on her son, he learned to respect and rely on order and reasoning. He dragged himself out of the violent, oppressive milieu that had prompted one of his uncles to murder another. My father desired discipline, culture, and independence, so he joined the military-a reasonable decision for a man who had no control over the time or skin he was born in.

My father may have been removed from the Bronx by the military, but it did not exempt him from the dangers of being a Black man in America. During his enlistment, a white lady at the base where he was stationed said she was raped by a Black man. My father was accused of the crime and imprisoned on the basis of no proof other than his race. To add to my father's misery and to act as a lesson to other Black soldiers, the white officers in charge assigned a Black officer to supervise him-a deliberate reminder that wearing a US military uniform did not conceal their race. It was a successful scare tool, similar to placing a Black supervisor on a plantation.

My father was embarrassed, but mostly terrified. He, like many Black guys, was terrified of arbitrary assault, kidnapping, or death. Perhaps most of all, he feared showing fear since he knew death was the guaranteed retribution for that violation. My father was eventually released, but he received no apology, support, or counselling. The sole explanation offered by the military was that they had caught the true perpetrator. He walked directly out of that prison to the top of a hill, armed with a government-issued rifle. He considered pressing the trigger, consumed by trauma and rage-and he was not thinking suicide.

Everything my father accomplished was done with surgical precision. His way of life was extremely austere: part military barracks, part Shaolin monastery. His kitchen was tiny but well-kept. His pantry was meticulously organised by size and type. In his house, there was no tolerance for excess or waste of any kind. There were no duplicates of anything: there was just one TV and one radio. Nothing more than a week's worth of clothing hanging in his closet. He didn't consider a bed to be properly made unless the sheets were so tightly tucked in that you couldn't bounce a quarter off its surface.

My father approached most things in an efficient and militaristic manner. He thought snacking was a trivial act. He would offer me one Ritz cracker if I was hungry while waiting for dinner. One. The appeal of that bright-red box was seductive, with its famous swirl of golden, sunflower-shaped crackers rising out of their wax covers. He'd pull out a tall column of crackers, remove the perfectly folded sleeve top, slide a single cracker from the stack, and gingerly offer it to me, as if it were a valuable treasure. He would then gently refold the paper, slide the stack back into the box, and place it back on the shelf, where it would remain.

I'd cup the buttery, salty, crunchy bliss to my nose, close my eyes, and take a long, pleasurable smell. I would take one teeny-weeny bite along the scalloped edge with care. I'd chew carefully, allowing the flavorful feeling to linger on my tongue. I would bite off another little piece of the golden treasure's edge, loving every grain of salt and crumb, making my one cracker last as long as I could. (Ironically, the box's motto was "there's only one Ritz"-and for me, there was!)

My father would have been called a hipster by today's standards. He went to Brooklyn Heights after the military, where he drove a classic Porsche Speedster and cooked real Italian cuisine in his kitchen. Oh, how I yearned for my father's cuisine! He cooked wonderful parsley meatballs and sausage and peppers, but his linguine with white clam sauce was sublime. The best Sundays smell like garlic in heated olive oil, boiling pasta, and the salty sea to me. Sundays were my favourite days. Those were the days I spent with my father, and I looked forward to our meals together the most.

Addie, my father's mother, was present one Sunday, which was unusual. I was probably no older than five years old. It started off like any other Sunday, with my father spending the entire day methodically making his specialty dish. He cleaned and shucked each clam, diced the garlic, and chopped the fragrant flat Italian parsley. It was a process, more of a ritual. I hadn't eaten anything all day, with the exception of a Ritz cracker (and I probably hadn't had a full dinner the day before; Saturday night at my mother's house can be a bit haphazard). I glanced at the pantry between reading and drawing and tummy rumbles. The freshness of my father's ingredients permeated the air. I'd waited all week, all day; all I needed to do now was hold off until dinnertime. I'd soon be savouring my favourite food.

I knew it wouldn't be long when I smelled the spaghetti softening in the boiling water. "It's time for dinner!"" Finally, my father sang. I leaped up and dashed to the kitchen's small Formica table. Addie, who wore a fantastic red wig and a red patterned caftan, was off on a tangent, narrating some narrative only adults would be interested in. I could scarcely keep my head up, as I'd probably begun to swoon and drool in anticipation of the delectableness that was going to materialise before me. I watched my father place the pasta on my dish, then scoop up the exquisite sauce and distribute it over the linguine with finesse. As he lowered the sizzling white platter in front of me, I watched his every action. It was finally time! Just as I was about to pick up my fork, Addie-who hadn't taken a breather in her story-whipped out a green container of grated Parmesan cheese and proceeded to shake its nasty, powdery contents all over my lovely fresh linguine.

Nooooooo!!!! In horror, I screamed. But it was too late; it had already covered my plate. That cheese was never on my father's white clam sauce! Where did it come from? Did she have it in her wallet?! I went to the restroom, closed the door, and burst into sobs, unable to suppress my horror and repulsion. "Roy, you'd better force her to eat that pasta." Make her consume that meal!" I overheard Addie defying my father. That was the only occasion I recall my father's flawless pasta being thwarted, and I believe it was the last time Addie joined us for Sunday dinner.

Words, according to my father, have meaning and consequently power. On a beautiful summer Sunday afternoon, I heard the faint jingle of the ice cream truck approaching my father's house. I let out an enthusiastic shout when I recognized the mystical music that promised so much pleasure: "Aaaaaa! The ice cream truck!" The song was now loud and clear, so I knew the vehicle had come to a halt someplace nearby. The sound of rushing feet and delighted squeals confirmed it-the ice cream man was just outside our door. My thoughts were racing. I have to leave! I was thinking to myself. He's getting ready to leave!

"Could I please borrow fifty cents?"" I nearly yelled at my father, on the verge of hyperventilating.

"Would you like to borrow fifty cents?" Or would you rather fifty cents?" He replied coolly and calmly.

A slight panic was setting in. "Uhhhh," I mumbled. I was at a loss for words. "All I knew was that I needed to get some money for the ice cream man.""

I wasn't thinking straight at the time. My father spoke in a patient, steady tone that just added to my excitement.

"There is a distinction between borrowing and owning. Are you requesting fifty cents from me?"

I was in a hurry and unprepared to make a decision, so I blurted out, "I just want to borrow fifty cents." I'll return it! Please!"

He dug into his pocket and pulled out two shiny silver quarters, which he placed in my nervous little palm. They felt like valuable diamonds, like the occasional Ritz cracker. I dashed through the building's doors, barely hitting the steps, and dashed to the vehicle like a gazelle being chased by a lion.

I had my ice cream, but my father made it obvious that I would be required to reimburse the money I had borrowed. I wasn't earning any money yet at seven years old, so I asked my mother for the quarters. She couldn't understand why my father would barter with his daughter, so she gave them to me. They had always had diametrically opposed parenting techniques. I maintained my promise and returned the money to him the next Sunday. The ice cream guy incident taught us not only about the meaning of words, but also about integrity and money management. My father was a man who had saved his very first dollar.

Being a single father was a novel concept at the time, so he wasn't prepared to organise girly playdates or pleasant, child-centred events. For the most part, I was just the kid who kept him busy and out of trouble as he cooked, cleaned, and tinkered with his car while listening to football on the radio. He also adored his Porsche. It was his one and only actual luxury. He acquired two of them throughout his lifetime, one before and one after having children, both used. His Speedster was supposedly always in need of repair, so he was constantly playing around in it.

The car was constantly being "prepared" for a comprehensive restoration. Because it was covered with grey primer rather than paint, it was a hazy, matte noncolor. I once questioned him why the car was such a dreary hue. He clarified that it was primer, but the original hue was sweet apple red. "Oh, you're going to paint it candy apple red one day?"" I inquired.

"They don't make that colour anymore," he stated categorically. I was perplexed. Why not just make it a different colour? But if it can't be the original hue, he'd rather it be none at all.

He was a patient man with the Porsche, spending hours with it and believing wholeheartedly in its exotic beauty and great performance. A soft-top convertible with two seats was really hip and sophisticated. He enjoyed the freedom of lowering the top and the closeness of having only one passenger. We would take long drives without any conversation. If there was a radio on, it was tuned to the news ("1010 Wins-you give us ten minutes, and we'll give you the world"). We'd occasionally sing one of those long, humorous folk songs, like "There's a Hole in the Bottom of the Sea."

We would go to Lime Rock Park, a racetrack in Connecticut, on occasion. It was a slightly more opulent experience than a standard NASCAR racetrack. There was a team led by Paul Newman, and world-class drivers such as Mario Andretti were regulars. I considered the racetrack to be tedious, but Alfred Roy enjoyed coming to the races and made all of his children join him. We youngsters could all agree on one thing: automobiles whirling around and around in a circle were not entertaining.

I was frequently merely about while he performed normal adult things on our drives or at the racetrack. I would be nearby, quietly reading or drawing as he listened to or watched football (which he loved and which I found terribly dull).

My father did have a few books in his house that were specifically for me. The one I recall most vividly was about a blind little Black guy. The cover was white with huge circles of red, orange, and yellow. It was colourful and presented the narrative of a youngster who perceived the world through touching and feeling forms rather than colour.

Stevie Wonder comes to mind when I think of that narrative. Reading that, I wondered whether this was why Stevie Wonder was able to create such vivid worlds and feelings in his songs: he was seeing without eyes; he was seeing with his soul. Stevie Wonder is by far my favourite and most respected songwriter. He is a talent; I feel he writes songs from a spiritual place. Because we didn't talk about it, I believe owning this book about the blind Black boy was one way my father sought to explain the principles of racism and perception to me. We didn't discuss our skin tones or body shapes.

My father placed a high value on perception. I once produced what I thought was a really brilliant cartoon while drawing alongside him on a calm Sunday afternoon. It was a photograph of our family with the comment, "They're strange. But they're fine." However, when I showed it to my father, he became very unhappy.

"How can you say we're strange?"" he insisted. His stern tone shook me, and I had no understanding why the concept had enraged him.

"I'm not sure. "I'm sure I heard it somewhere," I explained. "But they're okay," I added in my comic, which I felt was positive. It was a little sarcastic.

He responded, "Don't ever say that," with an earnestness that chilled me.

I had never tried to insult him; rather, I had hoped to delight him. That day, I felt awful. But the enormous burden he carried, his deep desire to be regarded as a full human being, I didn't learn about until much later—something I'm still trying to reconcile with.

I didn't have the words to tell him how strange I felt at the time. I didn't know how to express how I believed other people perceived us—as strange. Everything seemed strange to me. My hair was strange; my clothing were strange; my siblings and their pals were strange; my mother and all the shabby locations we lived with her were strange.

The Unitarian Universalist Fellowship struck me as an odd church. We began going when the family was still united. We'd go to this ancient mediaeval-style stone castle with thick walls and a towering tower, which was packed with what seemed like every odd person on the Island. It looked like the Church of Misfit Toys at a Renaissance festival to my little girl self. The former Jewish pastor had changed his name from Ralph to Lucky. "Are you Reverend Lucky?"" Okay. The teenagers would go up in the tower and do whatever teenagers did. Even as a child, I was aware that this was not my scene. But, despite being the only Black person there, my father felt accepted among the other outsiders, so he stayed at the fellowship indefinitely.

I don't think my father realised how different we were from everyone else in the neighbourhoods where my mother and I resided. It was strange to be living in a shack on top of a deli when everyone else was in a house. We resided in Northport's little business district, where there was a strip of retailers on the ground floor of a cluster of Victorian residences. They were small-town establishments: a bike shop, possibly a general store, and then the deli. A staircase next to the deli's door went up to a small, dingy railroad-style apartment where my mother and I lived with Morgan.

I had a room at the end of the corridor that was a little larger than a standard walk-in closet. The flat was modest, with pea-green carpeting on the floors and flimsy walls and doors; the sound of laughter and voices kept me awake at night. There were few things in that tiny space that gave me comfort. My father gave me a little ceramic bunny and a sweet molasses-coloured teddy bear named Cuddles, which I kept until it was destroyed many years later after a flood in a Manhattan apartment that was on top of a bar and nightclub (apparently, there are levels to living on top of establishments, and I have gone through them all).

Even with Cuddles by my side, I had regular nightmares, and it was in that bleak apartment that my sleep problems began.

I don't remember anyone else living nearby, and there were no other Black people for miles. Morgan was the only one with an Afro. After he got in trouble, my mother quietly ordered him to "stay in his room." Shortly after, the owner of the deli downstairs called my mother to tell her that he was seeing her son jump from rooftop to rooftop over the other establishments. Morgan had crawled out the window and onto the roof, attempting a daring escape. He went through a phase where he shaved his head bald and wore karate trousers with a snake casually slung about his neck. He'd roam around town like a punk ninja, full of rage, seeking to find a battle. Even without his hair, he was unmistakable.

My father didn't like it when I called the Careys strange, but strange things did happen to us. Alison would occasionally crash into the apartment like a meteor, and her and Morgan's buddies would hang there all night.

Alison scheduled me for entertainment one night. She'd taught me the song "White Rabbit" by Jefferson Airplane earlier that day. It was an unusual choice, to be sure, but I believed she loved it because the chorus "Go ask Alice" sounded similar to her name. All of the lights were turned off when I was led out to the living room to perform, and I was surrounded by burning candles and a circle of teenagers (along with my mother). I began the first verse while watching Alison's face for approval:

(One pill makes you larger, and one pill makes you small

And the ones that Mother gives you, don't do anything at all

Go ask Alice, when she's ten feet tall)

A song about tripping and doing drugs is not a normal (or appropriate) lyrical subject for a young girl. But I sang it because my older sister taught me. I loved learning and singing songs, but this one was full of frightening images ("the White Knight is talking backward /and the Red Queen's off with her head") and eerie nonsense ("the hookah-smoking caterpillar"-what?).

Of course, I was curious about the song and why I was singing it in the dark. While all the other kids my age were sleeping, I was roaring out, "Feed your head!" for a candlelit gathering of wannabe-hippie youths doing a pseudo-séance. Tell me that's not strange.

"See you next Sunday!" That was our specialty. My father and I exchanged that small promise with a wave each week as I left him to return to my mother's life. But as I grew older, my seriousness as a singer-songwriter began to quickly engulf my entire universe. I started working when I was twelve years old. My father did not see it or support it, owing to a lack of understanding.

Music as a career made no sense to him. When I mentioned composing poetry and singing, dad would change the subject to grades and assignments. He didn't see the concentration and discipline I was developing as an artist. He couldn't see how I was learning the trade by sitting in on jam sessions with accomplished jazz musicians with my mother and honing my scatting and improvisation talents. He had no idea how much time I spent composing, honing my ear, and researching popular music trends on the radio. Above all, we held opposing beliefs: I followed my heart, while he was motivated by his fear of not being accepted. I genuinely believed anything was possible after Nana Reese lay her hands on me and talked into my heart on that terrible and fortunate day. It felt genuine to me. Absolute. Nothing was possible, according to my father. He expected the world to forcefully refuse his demands, not the least of which was dignity.

Alfred Roy was a man who spent his entire life fearing humiliation and dehumanisation because of his identification. He believed that societal respect would be bestowed upon him as a result of his discipline, dedication, and performance in established institutional courses such as studies, service to your country, and respectable work. His other two children possessed all the characteristics of excellent students. He used to require that they produce all As on their report cards when they were younger, and they usually did (though he would occasionally wonder why each A wasn't accompanied by a plus). My one class in which I succeeded was creative writing, where I was consistently in the advanced groups. But I was terrible at arithmetic and couldn't connect with most other topics or material.

In their teens, the two prospective academics took horrible turns, fulfilling a Black father's worst nightmare. The youngster had been "institutionalised," placed in the fragile "care" of the state, the first stop on a perilous fast track to become a statistic. And the girl had already arrived at one, pregnant before her sixteenth birthday. And I, the non-wild child, eschewed the standard, "safe" road to a stable profession in favour of what he perceived as an improbable, unknown, and perilous path. My father was incredibly severe with my siblings, and they would frequently complain or make fun of him to my mother. However, in an attempt to shelter me from their harsh viewpoint, I frequently overheard mom tell them, "Don't say that in front of Mariah."

There were times when my father let me down. He went from being a divorced single father to a genuine bachelor after Alison moved out. He would sometimes fail to show up for our dates.

As a result, our Sunday habit became erratic over time. By that point, my music was consuming so much of my time and energy. I worked on it whenever I could. I was resolved to rise above my circumstances, to rise above the doubters, to rise above the miserable place my sister had fallen into, and to rise above my brother's angry dysfunction. I was going to rise above it all, even if it meant losing my father, my only stable family member. After spending one summer at a performing arts camp, the most my father ever did for my career was warn me about how dangerous and unreliable the entertainment industry could be.

Years later, I dialled my father's number and played "Vision of Love" from the recording studio, placing the phone receiver right next to the Yamaha speaker.

"Wow," he blurted out, "you sound like all three Pointer Sisters!" He wasn't a big music fan, so this analogy meant a lot to him. It signified that, in addition to the strong lead, he had observed all of the layers of backup singing. He was genuinely paying attention to my song. And I could see he was pleased with it as much as with me. It was extremely validating after all those years.

Despite my accomplishments, I was not immune to the perfectionism he had projected upon his previous children. He stated after I had won two Grammys in my first year in the profession, "Maybe if you were a producer you could win more, like Quincy Jones." The renowned Quincy Jones won seven Grammys the same year for his mammoth project Back on the Block, which spanned the whole history of Black American music and featured legends ranging from Ella Fitzgerald and Miles Davis to Luther Vandross.

I had done exceptionally well as a rookie artist (who had written her own popular songs), and here was my father, comparing me to perhaps one of the industry's biggest musical giants, with decades of experience and an unending list of accolades and honours to his credit! I was immediately transported back to my childhood, as if my two Grammys were two A's on my report card and he was wondering where the pluses had gone. I suppose my musical success worried him since he had no idea how I got there and appeared to have no influence over it. He didn't ask, and I didn't say anything.

"Next Sunday" gradually became a month of Sundays. I had to let go of our Sundays in order to create my own day in the sun.

Colouring Outside the Lines

My initial brushes with racism were like a reverse first kiss: each time, a bit of my purity was torn from me. A creeping stain was left behind, which permeated so deeply inside of me that I've never been able to entirely scrub it out. Not with time, not with fame or fortune, and certainly not with love. My first contact was when I was about four years old and in preschool. The day's exercise was to draw a portrait of our families. On the table was a stack of eggshell-coloured heavy-stock construction paper and little groupings of crayons for us to choose from. While I preferred singing and story time over colouring, I was enthusiastic about the assignment and resolved to give it my all. I hoped that if I did a good job, the teacher would add a gold-foil star sticker to my drawing.

I carefully selected my supplies, located a quiet area, and began working on the project. Our five-person family had not yet broken up. I had a father, a mother, a sister, and a brother for a brief time, and we were all living together in what seemed like relative calm. I wanted to make a family portrait that I was proud of. I wanted to draw everything that made each person unique-their outfits, their heights and proportions, their facial features-all the minute nuances that would bring my painting to life. Mother had long dark hair, and Father was tall. My brother was tough, and my sister had lovely ringlets. I wanted to document everything. As the mild, comforting aroma of Crayola wax floated through the room, the sound of crayons rubbing on thick paper formed a muted hum.

I was hunched up with my head down, nose almost touching the page, deep in thought over my masterpiece when I noticed a big shadow descend across my calm nook. I had a feeling it was one of the young student teachers standing over me. I had already developed a keen watch-your-back instinct at the age of four, so I immediately stopped moving my hand. Tension crept up and stiffened my small frame. I sensed danger and was immediately protective for reasons I didn't understand. I remained motionless until she spoke.

"How are you doing, Mariah?" Let's wait and see."

I lifted the paper toward her, relaxed a little, and proudly displayed my family photo in progress. The student teacher immediately burst out laughing. She was shortly joined by another young female teacher, who began to chuckle as well. Then a third adult joined in on the fun. The happy hump of children colouring with crayons came to a halt. The entire room had turned to look at what was going on in my little corner. From my feet to my cheeks, a mix of self-consciousness and discomfort surged up. The entire class was paying attention. I managed to speak despite the suffocating heat in my throat.

"Why are you laughing?" I inquired.

"Oh, Mariah, you used the wrong crayon!" one of them exclaimed through her laughter. You have no intention of doing that!" She was pointing to the drawing of my father.

As everyone continued to chuckle, I looked down at the picture of my family that I had painstakingly drawn. I'd coloured the skin of myself, my mother, my sister, and my brother using the peach crayon. For my father, I'd used a brown crayon. I knew my skin tone was more like animal crackers, my brother and sister were more like Nutter Butters, and my father's skin tone was more like graham crackers. But since they didn't have any cookie-coloured crayons, I had to make do! They pretended I'd used a green crayon or something. I felt ashamed and befuddled. What had I gotten myself into?

The teachers, still laughing uncontrollably, said, "You used the wrong crayon!" The entire bunch laughed, laughed, and laughed some more every time one of them made the proclamation. A crippling sense of shame was bearing down on me, but I managed to gently pull myself up, eyes burning and filled with hot tears.

"No," I informed the teachers as quietly as I could. I did not use the incorrect crayon."

Refusing to even address me directly, one of them snidely muttered to the other, "She doesn't even know she's using the wrong crayon!" The laughter and teasing seemed to go on forever. I stood there staring at them, trying not to puke from shame. Despite my sickness, I maintained my stare.

Eventually, the laughter subsided, and one by one, they moved away from the picture and from me. I noticed them across the room, hunched and whispering. They'd only ever met one of my five siblings: my mother, who dropped me off at school every day. She was the peach crayon colour. They had no notion, and no imagination, to imagine that the light toast of my skin, my bigger-than-a-button nose, and the waves and ringlets in my hair were the work of my father-my lovely father, the colour of warm maple syrup. His skin tone was a crayon hue they didn't have; brown was the closest I could get. It was the teachers who had gotten everything wrong. Despite their brutal and unjustified attack, they never apologised for humiliating a four-year-old kid in public, for their stupidity and immaturity, or for discouraging a four-year-old girl during colouring time.

My family of five had crumbled like cookies by the time I reached first grade. My parents separated, yet although living a short car ride apart, their Long Island neighbourhoods were worlds apart racially.

Becky was my best buddy in first grade. She was adorable and reminded me of the Strawberry Shortcake cartoon. She had enormous blue eyes, smooth strawberry-blonde hair that hung precisely straight down like heavy curtains, with reddish freckles scattered across her whipped cream-coloured cheeks. She reminded me of what tiny girls were meant to look like. She resembled the little girls who were treasured and protected; she resembled the little girl my mother may have had with a man her mother would have approved of.

Becky and I had a playdate at my house one Sunday, thanks to our mothers' planning. I was overjoyed since Becky and I had so much fun together. When Sunday arrived, my mother drove Becky to my father's place in whatever ragged automobile she was driving at the time. Becky and I jumped out of the car as we approached the brick townhouse. I took her hand and skipped up the stairs. My mother sat back and observed, which was unusual because she would normally have driven away. My six-foot-two-inch-tall, dashing father walked through the door with a hearty grin just as our feet reached the top of the stoop. He had the appearance of a movie star.

"Hiya, Mariah!" he exclaimed, greeting me as usual. Becky abruptly let go of my hand as he approached us. Her body stiffened and she erupted into tears like a bursting raincloud. Confused, I turned to my father for assistance, but I could see that he, too, was stopped and breathless, an ashamed expression distorting his strong face. My mind scrambled in disbelief as I struggled to absorb the unexpected and painful turn of events. Becky was in tears, and my father was in quiet agony: how had we arrived here in an instant?

I had no idea what to do. I was stuck there, motionless, for what felt like hours but was probably just moments. Becky was finally saved when my mother appeared behind us on the stairs. She tenderly placed her arm around the distraught little girl and walked her down the stairs and into the backseat of her car without even looking at me. My mother sped away with the strawberry blonde, without bothering to explain what had transpired. There was no solace, no mediation, no acknowledgement of my or my father's despair. In the aftermath of Becky's storm, my father and I stood quietly on the steps, waiting for the anguish to pass. Nobody ever discussed it again after that, but we never played together again, and the memory stayed with me for the rest of my life. And, believe it or not, her name was actually Becky.

When I was alone with my mother, no one ever questioned my ethnicity. They didn't dare to inquire about, or couldn't tell, the distinctions in our hues and textures. Becky, and most likely her mother as well, had undoubtedly imagined my father was similarly white, or perhaps exotic-but definitely not Black. That day on the stoop, I discovered unequivocally that I was not like the individuals I went to school with or who lived in my area. My father was completely different from them, and they feared him. But he was my people; I was descended from him. That day, I witnessed firsthand how their fear harmed him. And his pain really hurt me as well. But, perhaps most painfully, he saw that I saw their fear of him that afternoon. He knew that would have an eternal influence on me. He knew I'd never be able to regain the innocence that all children deserve.

<u>Hodel</u>

For me, singing was a type of escapism, while writing was a means of processing. There was some joy, but it was mostly about survival (and it still is). My mother, as well as my teachers, recognized my voice as a pure ability. My music teacher was a friend of my mother's, and she was fantastic. I was in a couple school plays as a kid, and I used to sing for friends at random events. When I was singing on stage (or anywhere), pretending to be someone else, I felt most like myself. Walking about by myself, coming up with melodies and singing to myself, was when I felt the most complete. To this day, I retreat to my private vocal booth to escape all of life's obligations and feel myself in my space, singing alone.

When I was in fifth grade, I was given the opportunity to attend an exclusive performing arts summer camp. This was a game changer! I could finally be around other young aspiring artists and polish my craft without being distracted by the noise and disarray at home. In the camp's production of Fiddler on the Roof, I was cast as Hodel, one of the five daughters. I lived for rehearsals. It was my favourite period and location. I was self-assured, swiftly learning the songs and researching their meanings. I enjoyed doing things over and over again, so practice came easy to me. I enjoyed seeing my performance improve with each try, discovering new and better ways to deliver a song.

My mother understood and encouraged my desire to learn music from an early age. She practised the Fiddler tunes with me at home, accompanied by her Yamaha piano. Even as a young child I was intrigued by the elements that comprised a wonderful song. And the musical's storytelling captivated me. I even made a "camp friend" amid the community of predominantly Jewish and rich kids. We became friends because we shared a passion for and seriousness about singing. We even had a similar appearance. She had thick curly, almost kinky hair and was Israeli. As a result, we both had tangled textures. We tried to match our outfits whenever possible, and we both wore the same pink onesie. People assumed I was a blond Jewish girl since they saw us together and observed some physical resemblance.

I admired Hodel because she fell in love with a revolutionary lad and travelled to the ends of the globe to pursue her dream. My big number came in the second act, "Far from the Home I Love." It was a good song for my breathy tone, and I recall singing it entirely emotionally. The song began with these beautiful, memorable lines:

(How can I hope to make you understand

Why do I do what I do?

Why I must travel to a distant land

Far from the home I love.)

My father was coming up to the camp for the opening night of the concert, and I was overjoyed. He was a sensible man who wasn't thrilled with my artistic proclivity, but he had unwillingly paid half of my expensive camp tuition that year. So, while he came to encourage me, he was also checking up on his investment. I didn't have the luxury of trying out other activities like the kids I went to school with-it was this camp or bust. So I knew I had to get everything I could out of it. There would be no hopping from tennis lessons to guitar lessons to dancing class. Even if we could afford it, I would never enrol in a dancing class. I was scared of dancing from a young age.

When Addie was visiting my father, she looked at my untamed flaxen hair and peach-crayon-coloured skin and declared, "Roy, that ain't your baby." "Girl, let me see you dance," she said, as if to prove her point. While I grew up in a musical household, I didn't do much dancing. My mother never danced, and I never saw my siblings dance. My father didn't start dancing until the late 1980s, when he began hustling classes.

Dancing, in my perspective, became a measure of Black acceptance, of belonging somewhere and to someone—of belonging to my father. That day, I didn't dance for Addie. After that, I didn't dance much. I couldn't shake the worry of not dancing "right" for my father. I stood there afraid to move, afraid that if I didn't dance well enough or moved incorrectly, it would indicate that my father wasn't my father.

As Hodel, I sang, smiled, pranced about the stage, and sang some more that day at camp. I sang in a distinctly lullaby tone. I was great, and everyone knew it. As I took my bow, I could hear thunderous clapping; it was like another kind of big music, giving me energy and hope. As I raised my head, I noticed my father's brightest smile. His smile was as bright as the sun. He approached the platform, his arms full of a large bouquet of sunny daisies tied with a lavender ribbon. He presented me the flowers with pride, as if they were a distinguished award. We were both too excited at first to notice that people were staring at us—and not in a positive manner, not because I had produced the best performance of the night. They were gazing because my father was the only Black man in the room, and I was his. That night, the teachers, parents, and other campers discovered that my father was a Black man, and I suffered the consequence. I received a huge ovation and flowers, but I never played a major role in another play at that camp again.

Light of My Life

"You've always been the light of my life."

When I was a kid, my mother told me this over and over. I wanted to be her beacon. I was determined to make her proud. I admired her as a performer and a working mother. I adored her and, like most children, I wanted her to be a safe haven for me. Above all, I was desperate to believe her.

However, ours is a tale of betrayal and beauty. Of love and rejection. Of survival and sacrifice. I've broken free from bondage countless times, but I fear a fog of melancholy will always hang over me, not only because of my mother, but because of our hard path together. It has caused me a great deal of grief and bewilderment. Time has taught me that there is no point in trying to defend individuals who have never tried to protect me. Motherhood and time have finally given me the confidence to face who my mother has been to me.

This is the most dangerous cliff edge in my opinion. If I can make it to the other side of this truth, I know there will be immense relief waiting for me. Those who have repeatedly injured me, from whom I have fled or walled off, are vitally significant in my tale, but they are not central to my existence.

Removing yourself from toxic individuals I care about was painfully hard, but after I mustered the guts (with prayer and professional assistance, of course), I just let go and let God. (I will add, however, that there is a significant difference between simple and easy. It's not going to be easy, sweetie.) However, there is no "artful" way to let go of my mother, and our relationship is far from straightforward. My relationship with my mother, like many other elements of my life, has been fraught with paradoxes and opposing truths. It's never been just black and white; it's always been a rainbow of feelings.

Our bond is a thorny web of pride, grief, guilt, gratitude, jealousy, adoration, and disappointment. My heart is linked to my mother's by a tangled affection. When I became a mother to Roc and Roe, my heart doubled in size; as my capacity for pure love grew, so did my ability to handle tremendous pain from my past. That is exactly what healthy, passionate love did for me: it highlighted the dark regions and excavated hidden hurt. The bright, clear light that my children's love has emitted now floods through every artery, cell, and dark nook and corner of my being.

Even after all this time, a part of me hopes that one of these days my mother will transform into one of the caring mothers I saw on TV as a child, like Carol Brady or Clair Huxtable; that she will ask me,

"Honey, how was your day?" before she gives me a report on her dog or bird, or asks me to pay for something or do something—that she will show genuine, sustained interest in me and what I'm doing or feeling. That one day she will recognize me. My mother will understand me one day.

To some level, I understand how my mother came to be who she is. Her mother had no idea what she was talking about. And her father never met her because he died while her mother was pregnant with her. She was the third child of a widowed Irish Catholic woman. My mother was dubbed the "dark one" because her hair was not blond and her eyes were a combination of brown and green rather than pure blue like her brothers and sisters'. Blue eyes were a symbol of white purity, and her mother's identity was built around being of 100 percent "pure" Irish lineage.

My mother grew up in Springfield, Illinois, in the 1940s and 1950s. It was the capital city of a state in the heart of the country. However, Springfield was also a hotbed of pernicious institutional prejudice. In 1908, a white woman was allegedly raped by a Black man (the same accusation leveled against my father and countless other innocent Black men), sparking a three-day riot by white citizens that resulted in the lynching of two Black men and the shooting of four white men by Black businessmen protecting their property. The Ku Klux Klan had a large presence in the city and the local government in the 1920s, when my mother's mother was coming of age, holding several key positions and defining the moral compass for the community. Springfield was an openly hostile city.

One of the few anecdotes my mother told me about her upbringing was about being in kindergarten and sharing her naptime mat with a Black youngster. The nuns at her Catholic school publically humiliated her for this. There was obviously a putrid repertoire of slurs for Black people in my mother's youth, but she also told me about the weird slurs and derogatory names they had for Italians,

Jews, and all "others" when no one else was present. She made me aware of the racism hierarchy in their white community. Surprisingly, even among her adoring Irish A social caste structure separated the "lace curtain Irish" from the "shanty Irish." The lace curtain Irish were portrayed as "pure," well-off, respectable, and "properly placed" in society (think of the Kennedys), whereas the shanty Irish were dirty, destitute, and ignorant. In this system, there was a desperate and terrible need for a slew of others to look down on. All "others" were inferior to the Irish, according to my mother's mother. But what about black? Black people were constantly at the bottom of the food chain. Nothing was darker than black.

My mother not only ignored her hometown's moral code; she rebelled against it, subsequently getting involved in the civil rights struggle. She was a liberal eccentric by the standards of her upbringing and family. She was curious about life outside of their small, white world. She was academically interested and attracted to culture, particularly classical music. She recalls hearing an aria while listening to a classical music channel on the radio one day. It was the most beautiful sound she'd ever heard, and she was determined to pursue it both inside and outside of herself. She opted to begin her journey in New York City, which seemed a million miles away from her family and the small-minded community in which they lived.

Patricia had high aspirations, many of which she fulfilled. She was gifted and determined. She won a music scholarship to the famous Juilliard School and went on to sing with the New York City Opera, making her debut at Lincoln Center. In New York City, my mother created an interesting, artsy, bohemian existence. She was in the downtown scene and dated a broad cast of men who would have humiliated her mother. Her mother, a devout Irish Catholic, would not approve of her dating anyone who wasn't lily-white. (Of course, the white supremacists of Illinois weren't enthusiastic about the Irish or Catholics-the WASPs [White Anglo-Saxon Protestants], as they were known at the time, were always looking for new people to put beneath them.) An Italian would have been an issue, and a Jewish man would have been a tragedy. If my grandma had known my mother had a torrid affair with a rich, older Lebanese man named François shortly before she fell in love with, and married, a man her mother couldn't even dream of. My grandfather. A lovely, complicated Black man. This was the worst thing my grandma (and her community) could have done to her and the family bloodline. Talking to a Black guy was frowned upon; befriending one was frowned upon; continuing to date one was frowned upon; but marrying one?

That was a heinous crime.

It was the pinnacle of humiliation. My mother's marriage to my father was a severe offence against her white heritage, punishable by excommunication.

Marrying a Black man carried a load of guilt for her mother, who grew up in a period and place where the KKK openly held enormous demonstrations and was involved in government. Her mother was raised not to drink from the same fountain, sit in the same seat, or swim in the same pool as Black people. She was taught and thought that Black people were filthy and that Blackness could be transferred. After all, the United States is the birthplace of the "one-drop rule," a racial classification system that states that everybody with a Black ancestor has at least one drop of Black blood.

According to my grandma, my mother's love for my father turned her into a bottom-feeder, procreating with the lowest human group and producing mulatto mongrels like me and my brothers. Needless to say, my grandmother disowned her daughter totally. She didn't tell anyone else in the family that her daughter was married to a Black man (and expecting a son). My mother was almost completely disengaged from her mother, save for a few irregular, hidden phone calls. She wouldn't return to her hometown for many years.

Even the most intelligent, caring, and progressive individual will struggle to overcome being entirely rejected by their mother. The demand for a mother's affection is far too primitive. My mother's soft landing spot was hardened like concrete by her own mother's ignorant, scared family and upbringing. Nothing, not even her marriage to my father and the birth of three beautiful children, could totally heal the profound wound of maternal rejection. I also doubt that loving a Black man and having mixed children will heal generations of white superiority beliefs, which my mother and her family were soaked in down to the white of their bones.

I've often questioned why my mother married my father despite her mother, family, and ancestry. What was her primary motivation? Was everything done in the name of unconditional love? They were never in a "we belong together" relationship. She never told me about their passion, and there was no physical proof of it: no photos, no poetry, no letters, no indication of a great love. (Well, there were three of them.) Perhaps my mother wanted to keep her history and memories of my father private, but I can't help but wonder if her marriage was a form of rebellion against her mother. Did she do it for the attention, for the drama? Over the years, I've heard my mother order her coffee "black, like my men." She's done it in front of me and one of her young Black grandsons, which is awkward.

To be honest, I'm not sure if my mother ever intended to marry and have children so young. I could understand her desire to establish a safety net, a new family of her own, and to continue blazing trails while abandoning her backward home and family. But I couldn't understand why she gave up her bright singing career to do so. I knew from the beginning that I didn't want to suffer the same fate; I couldn't let a man or an unanticipated pregnancy derail me. Seeing my mother and sister's diversions was a sad and painful warning. Seeing their dreams go up in flames burnt a warning into my head.

My mother released an album called To Start Again in 1977. But by then, she'd already had a tumultuous interracial marriage, three children, a divorce, and one child, me, who was still living with her. Did she expect a record label to come across her? This is one of many mistakes I saw my mother do as a child and saved in a file labelled "What Not to Do."

After my parents' divorce, time passed, and my grandmother ultimately permitted my mother to visit her with her granddaughter- but only her youngest granddaughter. I was a twelve-year-old girl who didn't understand why she had just invited me. In retrospect, I believe it was because I was blondish and fairly fair for a mixed kid. To the untrained eye, I didn't seem to raise much suspicion. I was too little to remember how my mother and her mother communicated, and I never knew what transpired between them at the time: Was Pat's mother sorry for disowning her daughter and keeping relatives from her? Did she consider her racism? Was forgiveness extended? I'm not sure. What I recall about her is that she was stiff and formal. She wore her hair nicely away from her face, with one large wave in the front. She wore black cat-eyed glasses on her stern face. Her house was not warm, and there was no smell. After my mother had put me to bed, I recall her entering the quiet, sterilised bedroom where I slept. She sat on the side of the bed in the dark and taught me the Lord's Prayer in hushed tones.

That's all I recall of my grandmother's visit. She died on my mother's birthday, February 15, in an odd turn of events. Strangely, my mother saw her as a saint after that. My mother was never a practising Catholic as an adult, yet she went to light a candle for her mother on that occasion for many years. It's strange how death may make individuals forgive those who have wronged them and their children.

It was only my mother and myself for the majority of my early childhood. We were continually on the run. She found us a spot along the water after a thorough search. She desired a more tranquil area where she could go for long walks with the dog and drive down the road to the beach. We moved into what she described as a "quaint cottage," but I subsequently learned that the entire neighbourhood referred to it as "the shack," which I thought was more realistic.

It was a small, wobbly structure with wavy faux-brick siding that had buckled from exposure to the elements. A layer of dismal misery crept through the floorboards and walls, which were covered with cheap "imitation of wood" panelling mixed with filthy flea-ridden carpeting. It was always gloomy inside, no matter what time of day it was. Prior to our arrival, the building had been abandoned and had become a hangout for youngsters who smoked, drank, and messed around. It stood off a rough, unpaved driveway of rubble and stones and faced a large white Victorian mansion, giving it the appearance of something the huge house had belched forth. It was labelled, as were we. My mother and I were the eccentric lady and her little daughter who lived in "the shack."

Marilyn Monroe's autobiography, My Story, begins with the chapter "How I Rescued a White Piano," in which she describes her journey to locate her mother's 1937 baby grand piano.

Gladys Monroe Baker, Marilyn Monroe's mother (born Norma Jeane Mortenson), spent her whole life in and out of psychiatric facilities. She was diagnosed with paranoid schizophrenia, an incurable condition that performs a violent dance with the mind, freeing it to lucidity for brief seconds before spinning it back into hellish delusion without warning. Marilyn spent the majority of her youth in orphanages, followed by a series of foster homes, as a result of her mother's failure to keep her sanity. Gladys and young Norma Jeane shared a little white cottage near the Hollywood Bowl for a few months during one of her rare healthy periods. A baby grand piano was their most valued asset in their small home. When her mother's illness resurfaced, driving her back into the darkness and into yet another institution, the meagre furnishings and piano were sold.

Following her transition into Marilyn Monroe The Movie Star, Norma Jeane revealed nothing about her childhood, her mentally ill mother, or her mysterious father. And, despite her transformation into a bright symbol, I suppose a part of her was still looking for an uninterrupted childhood, wishing for her mother to be whole. I can see how the piano came to represent a moment when she and her mother were in relative peace and harmony. Simple tunes and majestic compositions can come forth from a gloomy living room, a damp bar, a concert hall, or even a shack, and fill a dismal living room, a dank bar, a concert hall, or even a shack with joy and glory.

Marilyn set out to find her mother's piano. According to the account, while still a struggling model and actress, she spotted and purchased the piano at an auction and stored it until she was able to take it into her own home. It accompanied her to all of her homes. Marilyn's lavish Manhattan apartment with her third and final husband, renowned playwright Arthur Miller, was one of its final homes, where she custom-coated the instrument in a thick, shiny white lacquer to match the apartment's glamorous, angelic décor—"a world of white," as her half sister, Berniece Miracle, called it. "My happiest hours as a little girl were around that piano," Marilyn told me. When your upbringing was filled with worry and dread, as Marilyn's and mine were, I believe the romance of those lost pleasant hours is incredibly significant. I understood why she sought out, purchased, stored, and cared for the piano—so much so that I rescued it at Christie's auction in 1999. It is a gem and my most costly work of art. And now, Marilyn Monroe's white baby grand piano is the focal point, the showpiece, of my own opulent Manhattan apartment. Marilyn Monroe was my first vision of a superstar with whom I could connect on an almost supernatural level.

We had to make do with a lot of things when I was a kid, but one item my mother couldn't live without was a piano. We always had a piano, and I spent many joyful and formative hours with my mother around it. My mother would go over songs and scales with me, and I'd always hear her rehearsing her dramatic operatic scales. I used to sit at the piano and make up my own little tunes.

My mother was never wealthy, but one of her greatest contributions to my development was introducing me to a diverse range of individuals, particularly musicians. She supplemented her income by offering voice lessons at our place. Her practice was constant, but it was the jam sessions that I cherished the most. At my mother's bohemian hangout "by the bay," accomplished musicians would hang out and play music, and I would jam with them. The best thing about living with my mother was the live music. I was surrounded by people who loved music, but even more so, who loved musicianship—the love of the craft, the love of the process. My mother introduced me to the world of sitting in with musicians as a child, improvising, vibing, and singing.

I remember her singing from a Carly Simon songbook, which she would play all the time. She'd happily play a song for me to sing if I asked her to. She never forced me to sing or practice, but she always encouraged me to do so. She recognized my advanced musical ear early on. She arranged for me to take piano lessons for a brief time when I was five. Instead of reading the music, I would play "Mary Had a Little Lamb" by ear. "Never use your ear, never use your ear!"" My teacher would beg. But I didn't know how to avoid using my ear. I resisted the repetition and discipline required to learn to read music and play the piano since music was a gift of freedom in my world of scarcity, the one place I felt unconstrained. Hearing and imitating came naturally to me. This is one of the occasions when I wish my mother had pushed me and forced me to sit and endure.

My mother and her guitarist friend would also perform 1940s standards (of course, that's the era I adored, not only for the splendour but also for the melodies). She was a big fan of Billie

Holiday and would often sing her songs. I recall hearing my mother sing "I Can't Give You Anything But Love," which I learnt and we would sing together, with me immediately scattering, which I adored. It felt like I was catching the Holy Spirit as a tiny girl.

My mother and her musician friends taught me some jazz standards, and some of them took notice of my ear and natural ability. I used to sit with her and Clint, a piano player, when I was about twelve years old. He was a large brown teddy bear that liked to play with his ass. He would sit with me and work with me as if I were a serious musician. We were just two musicians working together when I sat with him and sang. He taught me jazz standards, and one of the first songs I recall learning was "Lullaby of Birdland," made famous by Ella Fitzgerald. Ms. Fitzgerald and all the jazz legends who laid such a fruitful musical foundation for performers of all genres will always hold a special place in my heart. It was not an easy song at any age, but it was beyond advanced for me at twelve. It was written for one of the most nimble jazz vocalists of all time, and features a complicated melody full of vocal shifts and variations. Learning to play and listen to live jazz helped shape my ear and creative circuitry. I was figuring out when to modulate and when to scat. Being exposed to jazz classics and a jazz discipline taught me to appreciate intricate modulations in a song and how to use them to portray emotion. (Stevie Wonder is the undisputed king of this.)

Songs are usually about emotion for me. My mother never took me to church, but jamming with jazz musicians was a spiritual experience. The place has a creative spirit that pours through it. You learn to sit and listen to what other musicians are doing, and you may be inspired by a guitar riff or the pianist's performance. It's miraculous lunacy when you're in a zone. It was always an incredible retreat for me, something I sorely needed and desired.

By the time I was eleven or twelve, my mother was taking me to a Long Island supper club to perform with her and other artists. On the main floor, there was a dining area where they served meals, and upstairs, there was live jazz. I was in sixth grade, sitting in with grown-up artists at all hours of the night, every day of the week. I'm not sure if my mother just wanted to be able to sing at night and not be locked in the shack—I mean "cottage"—with a kid, or if she was consciously training me as an artist, or if she wanted to show off her little protégée to her friends? I recall her encouraging me while I sang. I felt more welcomed (and natural) in the club at night with jazz musicians than with my classmates during the day—those kids who kept asking, "What are you?""those kids who judged me based on my appearance and had no idea what my life was really like." I'd always known that suburban Long Island wasn't for me. I was a fish out of water, and while I made it through, I knew no one there cared about me, and I knew I wasn't going to stay.

And my mother wasn't just any ordinary mother; she was a Juilliard-trained musician. We had a true connection through music, and without being pushy or becoming one of those obnoxious stage mothers or "momagers," she taught me the importance of believing in myself. "Don't say 'if I make it,' say 'when I make it.' Believe you can do it, and you will do it," she would say whenever I speculated about what I'd do "if I make it."

One of my biggest assets is my belief that I could become a successful artist. Around the same time, my mother entered me in a local talent show, where I performed one of my favourite songs, "Out Here On My Own" by Irene Cara.

"Out Here On My Own" felt like it reflected my entire life, and I enjoyed singing it that way—revealing a piece of my soul. And I won while doing it. At the time, I was obsessed with the film Fame, and Irene Cara was everything to me. I identified with her multicultural appearance (Puerto Rican and Cuban), multi textured hair, and, most significantly, her ambition and achievements. She was the first Black woman to win an Oscar for Best Original Song for "Flashdance... What a Feeling" (which she co-wrote) from the film Flashdance, making her the first Black woman to do so in a category other than acting. (She also received a Grammy, a Golden Globe, and an American Music Award for the song.) But "Out Here On My Own" was such a pure song that struck my heart, and I couldn't believe I had won a prize for singing a song I loved. It was the first time I'd been recognized as an artist. What a sensation.

It wasn't just music that my mother introduced me to. She had friends who treated me like family, which helped to compensate for the shabby locations we lived and the untidy appearance I frequently exhibited.

My mother had a friend named "Sunshine," who was small and rather large, but had a kind and loving heart. She wore her hair in two long ponytails like Carole and Paula from The Magic Garden (a popular local kids' TV show I liked in the 1970s and early 1980s hosted by two young, hippie-esque women with a pink squirrel sidekick who sang folk songs and told stories). Sunshine had two elder sons and no daughters, so she was drawn to me, particularly because of my disordered and neglected appearance. She would frequently bring me cute, girly outfits she had created herself. She dressed me in a white embroidered shirt, a blue skirt, white tights, and Mary Jane shoes for my sixth birthday. She even got my hair to fall into pigtails (maybe because she was Jewish and had textured hair). My birthday crown fit perfectly on top. She even bought me a lamb-themed birthday cake! A lamb! It was one of the rare moments as a child when I felt gorgeous. Sunshine took great care to ensure that I appeared presentable and cute. She was always thoughtful and sweet to me. Years later, when I was starting junior high, she stopped by with some outfits that I thought were too infantile for me. I rejected them angrily, in the callous manner of an angry adolescent. To this day, I regret being so cruel to such a thoughtful caregiver—one of only a handful in my entire life.

I tried my utmost to accept all of my mother's bad luck with men. I even made an attempt to impress them. (Some names have been altered to protect the jerks.) Stories about a certain man in my mother's life just before my father loomed large in our household. We knew his name was François, that he was Lebanese, and that he was wealthy. Despite her many qualities, my mother, like many women of her generation, believed that a man was her most dependable source of protection. The time span between her connections with François and my father was short; it was even claimed that there had been some overlap, raising the possibility that Morgan was not my father's kid. Drama.

My mother and François reconnected after my father's divorce, and she planned an epic reunion with "the rich man who got away." My mother enthralled Morgan and me with the fantasy that a wealthy, exotic man would come and sweep us up out of our run-down digs, and we would be set for life—all we had to do was impress him. That's something I could do, I reasoned. Could my mother and I sing a song at the piano? While my mother and François were out on their big date, I put together the finest little dress I could to greet him. I was scared because my mother desperately wanted to be rescued, and I wanted to be in a beautiful, safe place as well. The stakes were really high.

When my mother and François returned, I was home alone (I was home alone a lot as a child). I dashed to the door, determined to do my part to make this relationship work for my mother. François was the first to arrive. He was a tall, powerful older man dressed in a dark suit with sharp, enigmatic features. "Hello!" I began cheerfully, possibly with a curtsy for dramatic effect. "Stop talking!" he yipped. "Where has my son gone?!?""

The intensity of his words sucked all of my enthusiasm away. He was terrifying. I was only a child when this large stranger walked into my house, dismissed me, and yelled at me. I sobbed my way into my mother's bedroom. She tried to console me, but I was enraged. I'm not sure François ever saw Morgan (who had our father's Black characteristics all over him). But, needless to add, no rich, heroic man saved us that day; no man ever "saved" us.

Most of my mother's men made me uncomfortable. Leroy, her older Black partner, tried to "protect" us from Morgan during one of his more violent outbursts by declaring, "I got my piece," and brandishing a revolver. Consider this: your mother's boyfriend is carrying a pistol and threatening to shoot her adolescent kid, your brother. Unfortunately, it did make me feel safer; Morgan had become a frightening presence to me by that point.

My mother's guys, on the other hand, were not all horrible. Nothing or no one is ever entirely negative. Henry was a wonderful man in my mother's life. He was my personal favourite. He was around ten years my mother's junior and a horticulturist. He drove an ancient red pickup truck prepared for the field, with his numerous gardening tools, tree trimmings, mulch, and other materials protruding from the rear. He was an expert in his field. He was very well informed and grew magnificent plants that towered over me (mostly illegal species at the time). He also developed a stunning Afro that seemed to float about his head. My mother and I moved about a lot with Henry, but for a while we lived in a modest house on a big estate where he was the gardener. The setting reminded me of a plantation, and we lived in the modern equivalent of the servants' quarters. But Henry's house was nicer than most of the others we'd lived in, and it provided me with a brief respite.

When we lived there, I was in third grade, and Henry constructed me a swing on a big, old tree beside what appeared to me to be a garbage-filled mini-mountain. He brought home two rescue kittens one day, one for me and one for him. I preferred him; he was orange and had a unique personality. He eventually became my. He grew to be enormous and squishy, and his name, like the emblem, was

Morris. I'd sit on my lap and swing with him. We adored each other. I confided in him whenever I had a particularly difficult day at school, which was very frequent. I never blended in with the youngsters, who were mostly white and lived mostly in the estates in that area. They informed me that I was the child of the hired help's girlfriend. I told Morris about my problems. Even if I had friends, I wouldn't have wanted them to know I lived near a landfill. When I was incredibly unhappy after a large fight with my mother, I ran out of the house, grabbed my cat, and went to my place. While swinging over the garbage mound with Morris in my lap, the stench of rotting food blowing across my face, I told myself I would never forget what it was like to be a child—a scene I recreated years later in the "Vision of Love" video. (With the exception of the rubbish, I intended to seem nostalgic rather than dismal.)

I liked Henry since he was an Aries like myself. We'd dance, and he'd lift me up and spin me around. He showed me glimpses of what a carefree little girl's life may be like. Henry was generous enough to cover the cost of my second year of performing arts summer camp. I recall his mother, who worked for Estée Lauder and was an excellent cook. She laid out a beautiful soul food spread one day, finishing with a German chocolate cake I'd never had before. It was a delectable, warm, gooey, handmade pile of joy. But, with all that affection, there was also darkness. Henry was a Black Vietnam soldier who suffered greatly as a result of the ramifications of his identities. I assume dad had post-traumatic stress disorder (PTSD), and I was aware of his psychedelic drug use even as a child. I believe the repercussions from his wartime and racist experiences was the main cause of his and my mother's divorce.

When I got home one day near the end of my third-grade school year, my mother was enraged. "We can't stay here any longer," she declared. We had to leave right now."

She had already packed our belongings and placed them in her car.

Henry was sitting in the middle of the kitchen in a chair. I could see the bold shadow of his Afro with the lights turned off. In one of his hands was a long double-barreled shotgun. "You're not leaving me," he stated calmly, staring down at the white linoleum floor. "I'm not going to let you guys go." He never raised his head or voice and appeared to be in a trancelike state.

"I'm not going to let you guys go," he told them. "I'm going to chop you up and put you in the refrigerator and force you guys to stay here," he shouted, as I dashed into the car. My mother cranked up the engine.

"Morris!" I yelled. "I've got to go get Morris; he's still in there!"" I jumped out of the car, terrified. I was very set on getting my kitty. That cat meant too much to me; he had unconditional affection.

"Be careful," my mother warned as she let me back into a residence where an armed man had just threatened to hack us up. (Henry had never hurt me, and perhaps she thought he wouldn't now, but still.) I had to pass through the kitchen with Henry and the shotgun to search the other rooms for Morris. I grabbed him up in my arms, dashed out of the house, and hopped in the car when I finally found him. My heart was racing as we accelerated away. "Hallelujah, Morris!"" I exclaimed triumphantly.

I had no idea what happened between her and Henry, and I had never seen him since that day. "'Vision of Love,' by Mariah Carey," came blasting through his old radio many years later, while he was cruising down the road in his identical vintage red pickup. He rolled down the window and cried out into the open air, "She made it! She did it!" I really hope Henry made it as well."

My mother did attempt to give us moments now and then. She would put money aside so that we could do things like go to dinner in New York City. And it was on these things that I developed an appreciation for "the finer things." I recall one night when we were coming back from the city. Looking out the back window at the New York City skyline, I thought to myself, "This is where I'll live when I grow up." I'd like to have this perspective.

I was constantly aware that we lived in slum areas among other people's magnificent houses in the suburbs. I never imagined marrying and living in a beautiful white Victorian mansion, or even a nice tiny house like my guncles. However, I had grandiose plans. I recall witnessing Joan Crawford's immaculate mansion while seeing Mommie Dearest. That's exactly what I'm looking for, I reasoned.

I even thought I could outdo its splendour. Even back then, I imagined myself living in a mansion or more since I knew I would achieve my goals. And when I saw the New York skyline, which resembled a massive silver crystal studded with rainbow gems, I imagined myself living somewhere where I could see it. And I do as well. I can see everything plainly; from the balcony of my downtown Manhattan penthouse, I can see the entire city. I went from swinging over garbage to singing in a house in the sky as a consequence of a lot of hard work.

So, absolutely, my mother's exposure to beauty and culture provided me with support and lasting lessons that benefited both my work and what is good in me. But my mother also produced ongoing instability, which resulted in trauma and tremendous despair. It has taken me a lifetime to summon the strength to confront my mother's stark dichotomy, the beauty and the beast that coexist in one person—and to know there is beauty in all of us, but who loved you and how they loved you determines how long it takes to recognize it.

Looking back, I can see that there was a lot of neglect in my early years. For one thing, there were the people my mother let around me, especially my violent brother, my disturbed sister, and their shady associates. And I was often a mess, which I feel was due to my mother being clueless (in the idea of being bohemian) rather than malevolent. However, when I was approximately fourteen years old, I sensed a change in our relationship. "Somebody's Watching Me," by Rockwell, played on the radio one night as we were riding in the "Dodge dent," as she called it. It was a tremendous international hit for Motown Records at the time, and I adored it, owing partly to Michael Jackson's vocal performance on the hook. My mother broke out into Michael's famous section of the chorus while we were driving and bopping along to the song. "I always feel like / Somebody's watching me."

I turned my face to the window to hide my laughter as she sang it in an exaggerated, operatic style. It's a very eighties R&B hit, with the hook sung in Michael Jackson's flawlessly smooth hallmark style, so hearing it performed like Beverly Sills (a popular Brooklyn-born operatic soprano from the 1950s to the 1970s) was rather amusing to my teen singer's ears.

Mother, on the other hand, was not amused. She slammed the volume down on me, her brownish-green eyes narrowing and hardening to stone.

"What's the big deal?"" she yelled. Her seriousness soon gobbled up the moment's playfulness. "Um, well... that's just not how it goes," I faltered. She gazed at me until all lightness disappeared. "You should only hope that one day you become half the singer I am," she replied almost growlingly. My heart fell.

What she said still haunts and pains me to this day. I'm not sure if she meant to cut me down to size or if it was just her injured ego speaking; all I know is that those words pierced my chest and were buried in my heart.

These words were in my heart in 1999, when I was recognized and admired for my voice and compositions by two of the world's top opera artists. I was asked to perform with Luciano Pavarotti in "Pavarotti & Friends," a distinguished yearly fundraiser performance for children in war-torn nations organised by the great tenor in his birthplace of Modena, Italy. (Did you know Spike Lee directed the concert on television?) It's a historic town famed for producing beautiful sports cars like Ferraris and Lamborghinis, as well as balsamic vinegar—and I'm sure whatever indulgences the maestro needed were imported. I brought along my mother and my adorable young nephew Mike. I was honoured and delighted to be able to take her on a luxurious trip and present her to one of her idols. My mother stood there in a strapless pale-pink silk taffeta sheath gown, watching me share a huge outdoor platform with one of the greatest and most famous opera singers of all time. Not only did we sing together, but he also sang my song: Pavarotti sang an Italian rendition of "Hero" with me in front of the entire world. To show my mother.

Then, in May 2005, I met Leontyne Price (the first Black woman to become a prima donna at the Metropolitan Opera and the most awarded classical singer) at Oprah's illustrious Legends Ball, which honoured twenty-five African American women in art, entertainment, and civil rights. On Friday, the "legends" were greeted by the "young'uns," who included Alicia Keys, Angela Bassett, Halle Berry, Mary J. Blige, Naomi Campbell, Missy Elliott, Tyra Banks, Iman, Janet Jackson, Phylicia Rashad, Debbie Allen, myself, and many more.

Throughout the incredible weekend, we young'uns paid tribute to the legends for their outstanding achievements. "Oh yes, Leontyne and I had the same vocal coach," my mother would often boast, and here I was hanging out with her (at Oprah Winfrey's house, no less)! Madame Price recalled my mother and recognized my talent.

On the day after Christmas that year, I received a letter from her on the most magnificent, thick, eggshell-coloured stationery:

("You are the crown jewel of success in the difficult, demanding business of performing arts." It went on to state, "Achieving your level of success as a multi-dimensional artist is an outstanding measure of your artistic talent."

It was a pleasure to visit with you during the Legends Weekend and to tell you in person how much I admire you and your artistry. Your creativity and performances are superb. You present your compositions with a depth of feeling that is rarely, if ever, seen or heard. It is a joy to watch you turn all of the obstacles you faced into stepping-stones to success. Your devotion to your art and career are praiseworthy. This brings you a standing ovation and a resounding Brava! Brava! Brava!)

Dead

I suppose to my mother, I wasn't half the vocalist she was, but I was the entire singer and artist I was.

This was my first insight into how a mother's mistaken comments may truly harm a child. What a difference a little giggle from her would have made. Whatever had previously bound us together, a frail mother-daughter tie, was obliterated in that moment. There was a noticeable shift: she made me feel like the enemy, a menace. A new tie grew in lieu of our prior one, a rope connecting us via common biology and social obligation. My mother did not kill my ambitions of achievement that day; my faith had become too strong by then.

Having somebody you care about be professionally jealous of you comes with the territory of success, but when the person is your mother and the envy is shown at such a young age, it's very devastating. I was going through a lot at the time, and for her to show her vulnerability to me in that way was hurtful. I'd already endured years of anxiety about my physical safety. Despite the fact that it was a quiet, brief moment, it was the first major blow in a long series of instances when individuals close to me tried to put me down, put me in my place, underestimate me, or take advantage of me. But she was the most damaging because she was the most necessary. My mother was her name.

Dandelion Tea

She dubbed herself Dandelion, after the hearty, bright-yellow wildflower with little tooth-shaped petals that signals the arrival of spring. After blossoming, the petals dry and the head transforms into a ball of lacy dust feathers containing seeds. According to folklore, if you close your eyes, make a wish, and blow the feathery parts into the air, your wish will scatter and come true. The English refer to them as Irish daisies. And the tea brewed from the root and leaves is often thought to have medicinal properties. However, these wildflowers can be a nuisance, killing beautiful flowers and sprouting grass—weeds that must be pulled and thrown.

My older sister seemed to live on the wind when I was a tiny girl. She was constantly somewhere else. Childhood memories of her flash across my memory like lightning and thunder. She was exhilarating, but unpredictable-her torrential storms usually brought with them unavoidable destruction.

The gaps between my mother, father, their first daughter, and myself are vast. Unlike her, I never spent a considerable amount of time growing up as part of an interracial family. The majority of my encounters were with one parent at a time, either my mother or my father. I don't remember them as a happily married couple. I find it strange that they were married at all, not just because of their ethnicity, but because of how different they were as people. Prior to my birth, the Carey family had a Black father, a White mother, and a mixed son and daughter. People would notice them as they walked down the street. This renegade Carey four was subjected to the remarkable ignorance and hatred of a society that was utterly unable to receive or accept them. The Supreme Court ruling in Loving v. Virginia, which overturned the rule against interracial marriage in the United States, would not come until three years after my mother and father's marriage. Because of the animosity from their neighbourhood and country, our parents encouraged Morgan and Alison to refer to them as "Mother" and "Father," presumably in the expectation that the formality would elevate their status to respectable status. My parents seemed to believe that if neighbours or other spectators heard their daughter and son say, "Good morning, Mother" or "Hello, Father," they would not find them repulsive.

Morgan and Alison were gorgeous youngsters who were very close as children. Alison had skin the colour of rich butterscotch pudding, thick, deep, dark curls, and eyes to match. She was highly brilliant and inquisitive, and she adored learning. I was informed she received outstanding marks, went to good schools, and enjoyed music as well. But she witnessed the discomfort and hostility hurled at her and her oddball Black and white family firsthand. She witnessed their neighbours feeding raw meat laced with broken glass to their dogs, as well as their family car being blown up. She saw things within the family that a child should never witness, and I will never know. I do know that what she went through harmed and wrecked her girlhood.

She was fully aware when the family unit disintegrated and our parents turned on each other; she felt the full sorrow of a family disintegrating. She also witnessed another daughter join the clan, shattering the symmetry and altering her position as the sole girl and youngest. I was the new addition. My mother and father tore themselves apart to survive separately when they could no longer live together without mentally abusing one another. For the rest of our lives, the three of us children would be tortured with pain, bitterness, and jealousy.

Both Alison and Morgan thought I had it easier than they did. Our father was harsh with them. He wasn't tough with me because I was just three or four years old when we were all together. During one of their many confrontations, I vaguely recall my mother shrieking at him, "This one is mine! You're not going to beat this one." I was her youngster. When my siblings were growing up, she frequently stated that she "didn't have the strength" to confront my father's aggression.

I only recall one occasion when we all ate dinner together. It was a "restorative dinner," with my parents attempting one more time to see if we could all get along and be a family. I started singing as we were all sitting around the table.

My father once observed, "Children should be seen and not heard."

The entertainer in me took that as a cue to get up from the dining table, move a few feet to the living room area (which was in plain sight and well within earshot), stand on top of the coffee table, and sing at the top of my lungs. Alison and Morgan lowered their heads, cowering before our father's fury, which they were confident would ricochet throughout the room. But my mother gave him a look, and he remained silent. My sister and brother were taken aback. I was not hit, screamed at, disciplined, or even brought to a halt. They would never have dared to challenge our father. It's no surprise they despised me.

Needless to say, the dinner did not come to our rescue. The divorce was unavoidable. My mother and father made the final decision to divorce before everything was destroyed. I recall being taken to our neighbours' house and being given popcorn as my family was discussing the deconstruction of the Carey's next door. My father and brother could not live together due to a court order following multiple violent incidents with police. Morgan had been admitted to Sagamore Children's Psychiatric Center, an institution for severely emotionally disturbed children and families in crisis. Morgan was a disaster. I also heard that a psychiatrist had concluded that Alison, who had a gift for inciting and pushing Morgan to his breaking point, was a big contributing element in Morgan's behavioural difficulties. Alison is really intelligent. Morgan was forced to live with my mother, who had made it apparent to my father that he would not accept me. Alison was scattered as a result of this.

I've heard Alison say that she felt pushed aside by my mother, who plainly loved Morgan and me more than her. My mother has also stated that Alison opted to live with our father because she felt awful for him and didn't want him to be alone. Both of their points of view are probably correct. I was too young to fully comprehend.

I'm not sure what it was like for my sister to live with our father, just the two of them, damaged and angry. Under their roof, it must have been dangerously claustrophobic, with a constant clash of sentiments of desertion and hostility toward my mother. They had no true space to resolve their issues and no chance to heal. Order and obedience were my father's attempts to make sense of the chaos of society and the shambles that had become his family structure.

The child in his care was a bitter, shattered adolescent girl, and he lacked the ability to deal with her dysfunction and hurt. My father and Alison eventually became friends, united in their dislike for my mother. I believe they also bonded because of the inevitability of their Blackness.

Alison, predictably, resorted to boys and sex to fill the family-sized hole of rejection in her heart. When Alison was fifteen, she met an attractive Black nineteen-year-old military "man," and she became pregnant. Our mother desired that she have an abortion. Our father informed her that if she married, she could have the baby. The young guy was stationed in the Philippines, and Alison followed him there with our father's consent, where they married. I remember sitting on the bed with her in her room at our father's house before she departed. I recall her room having a shelf of books and a shelf of fancy dolls-the ones with large, poofy lace quinceanera-type outfits. I'd glance up at those dolls, far out of reach, there for display rather than play.

I was staring at them when she said, "There's a baby in there." Where is the baby? In her tummy? I was too young to understand what she was saying. I didn't know anything about Alison at the time.

I'll never forget her unusual baby and bridal shower at my mother's house. They put a tiny girl on the cake-a doll, not a grown woman, but a baby doll with dark brown hair like my sister's. Everything was very perplexing to me. I was a tiny girl, wondering if this was a baby-coming or a girl-going party. I couldn't determine if it was a happy or sad occasion. My mother was pacing and irritated. My teen sister had a bloated belly and kept pointing to it and exclaiming, "There's a baby in here; look, there's a baby in here." And there was this strange cake with a doll on it. What was a tiny child supposed to make of all of this?

So, for a long time after that, I thought to myself, "Okay, so I guess fifteen is when people have kids and get married."

It distorted my perception of reality. It did, however, focus me. That was not going to be me, I promised myself. My feeling of self-worth, or rather, self-preservation, was born during that farewell/bridal/baby shower. I decided I would never be promiscuous again. This pledge to live a different life caused me to become a very conservative individual. I knew then, when I found myself an auntie at the age of eight, that Alison's path would not be mine. My sister was gone for several years after the last slice of baby-bridal cake was gone.

What happened to her in the Philippines will never make sense to me. But I do know that when mom left my father's house, she left the rest of her frail childhood behind.

Alison returned to Long Island after a few years in the Philippines. She was twenty years my senior, and I was about twelve. Whatever had occurred to her there, on Long Island, or in a back room somewhere had taken its toll. My big sister, the super-smart, gorgeous girl with the dark hair, had hardened into a strange kind of absence. Something, or a combination of things, must have happened to her to cause her to exchange her body for money and drugs, as she did for years. There was so much I didn't know back then, but there was also so much I should never have found out, especially so young. The years that separated us may have been centuries.

When Alison returned, she drifted from place to place and man to man, occasionally crashing with us at my mother's house in between the many odd relationships she accumulated and discarded. There was one elderly man-I'd say he was around sixty years old. He sported only half a head of grey hair. He was pleasant to my mother and would occasionally stock our refrigerator, so I assume she trusted him? Alison and my mother were having one of their numerous epic disagreements at the shack one evening, and for some apparent reason, Alison took me to this elderly gentleman's house. I remember little of his house or that night because Alison put me down on a light-brown couch and gave me a little chalky ice-blue pill with a crease etched down the middle and a glass of water when we arrived.

"Here, take this," she instructed.

I accepted it. Within minutes (I believe), I was forced down into a region beneath sleep, and I couldn't pull myself out. I'm not sure how long I was unconscious. I felt as if I'd been absorbed into the couch (which is why I recall the colour). It was terrifying.

Alison gave me a whole Valium when I was twelve and probably weighed eighty pounds soaking wet. I'm not sure why my sister drugged me. I'm not sure why my mother allowed me to accompany her and this man. Perhaps they both wanted me out of their hair for the evening, but in her hands, my life was in danger. This wasn't the first time she could have really wounded me that year, but it wasn't the last.

Alison could be crazy and spontaneous even though she had previously married, given birth, divorced, gone hundreds of miles away, and done terrible things by her twenties. The worst was yet to come between us, so I was really grateful for her sporadic visits to my mother's place. On her good days, she was a brilliant burst of vitality in our often-dark small house. She appeared mature, with a hollow kind of glamour. She was more interested in me as a tween than as a young girl. She focused on the obviously neglected outside of me, swooping in and correcting my horrible attempts to make myself lovely, which meant everything to a twelve-year-old. She took me to acquire a toner for my hair after I mistakenly turned it all different shades of unsightly orange. She took me to a place that enhanced the beauty of my brows. She went bra shopping for the first time. She and I would make concerted efforts to appear normal. We were pretending to be sisters, I thought.

Even though I was young, I could tell my sister was doing bad things. I mean, she had a beeper, and back then, only drug dealers, rappers, and physicians had beepers. She had a lovely manicure-bright pink nail paint with rhinestone accents. She once dropped me off in front of my mother's house with a sharp pink nail tip bathed in white crystal powder and put it up to my face, saying, "Just try it, just try a little bit; who cares?"

I knew it was cocaine, and it terrified me. I'm glad I didn't take the sniff. I played it off and said casually, "No thanks!" "Bye; I'll see you later." I shudder at the thought of what may have occurred if I'd walked into her trap and then into that house. I'm not sure what would have occurred if I'd snorted cocaine right before visiting my mother, or ever.

It was all a set-up. Alison began introducing me to her friends, and I began to look forward to our covert outings—though, despite the initial glitter and excitement, it was a terrifying moment in my life. Even though it happened a long time ago, it still gives me nightmares. Alison did not choose how her life began, and I know she experienced trauma as well. She appeared to have turned totally away from the light.

She told me one day that it was time for me to meet her fantastic boyfriend, John, and the other girls she hung out with, about whom she'd been telling me stories. John was tall, with green eyes, a thick, fluffy Afro, and a powerful personality. Christine, a seventeen-year-old runaway white girl, Denise, an older woman-"older" meaning she was probably twenty-eight-and my sister, then in her early twenties- all shared a house with John. Christine had a sophisticated air about her, yet she still seemed like a small child to me. Her pale skin was freckled with tan, and she wore her medium-blonde hair softly down to her shoulders, which were long and slim like the rest of her body. She could have been in a teen film, but instead she was in that house. She had been harmed.

John's place was nicer, brighter, and cleaner than mine. They were sitting on a brand-new couch. I had access to a television and could watch any shows I liked. They had every foodstuff imaginable. They served Juicy Juice. At home, we couldn't afford any of that. My sister visited me a few times and stocked the refrigerator with items I enjoyed. This contributed to my perplexity regarding our connection. She appeared to care at times, but her motivations were never obvious. Was she being a good big sister, or was she instilling in me a desire for what I knew I could have at John's house all the time? It was deception disguised as affection.

My sister warned me not to tell anyone, especially my brother, that I was going to the house where she lived with John. She informed me that my brother disliked him since he had defeated him at backgammon. I was so young and naive at the time that I thought their hostility was over a board game, not a prostitution and drug enterprise. So no one knew, and no one could defend me. Abusers love to prey on dysfunctional homes because the exposed children are easy prey. Of course, it's obvious to me now that the fun house was a whorehouse. My sister, I believe, was the hustler and talent scout. But I had no notion at the time; after all, I was only a twelve-year-old girl. It was literally like giving a kid candy, only instead of candy, it was a hair rinse, a bra, and a Juicy Juice box.

John, my sister, and I would carpool to the city. I recall a day when we were driving somewhere and the radio was playing a song he liked. While my sister and I smiled at his strangled singing, he yelled out the lyrics. They let me smoke cigarettes in the car's backseat. I felt calm and liberated.

We'd head to IHOP for pancakes. I went to Adventureland and played Pac-Man. I felt like someone's adorable little sister in those moments. I was enjoying all of these exciting adventures and thinking to myself, "I finally know what it's like to have a big sister who is permanently in my life." And I like this easygoing John. This was what I'd been looking for. I was beginning to feel a feeling of security, as if I had something like a normal family and was making my way toward somewhere I belonged.

But strange and perplexing things began to happen swiftly.

The closer I got near my sister, the more obvious her shattered bits were. She had discreetly acquired my own phone line, which she was the only one who could call me on. She'd have these frantic periods of drug-induced hysteria and phone me late at night, right in the thick of one. I'd talk her down from the cliff, then attempt to sleep, get up early in the morning, and finish seventh grade. Nobody at school knew that just a few hours before, I had restrained my suicidal big sister. Suicide became a recurrent threat she communicated with me in the early morning hours before I headed to the school bus stop.

The calls then stopped for a while. Finally, Alison called to say she and John were on their way to pick me up. I was excited to think of the three of us riding, laughing, smoking, singing, and playing together again. But John arrived by himself.

We started driving, but there was no music or chatting. It was not enjoyable, and I had the impression that something was wrong.

"Where is my sister?" I finally inquired. "When are we going to get her?"

John kept his gaze forward, assuring me, "Oh, she'll be here later." I was seated in the front seat, and I could see the revolver against his thigh.

I stopped at a card game and a drive-in movie with John and his gun. Rooms where grown men play in the dark have a certain aspect, feel, and smell to them. It was dark and crowded. The air was thick with old menthol cigarette smoke and unsaid perversions. There were no beautiful things. It was difficult for me to see and breathe.

I'm not sure how many men were present; I'm not sure how many guns, how much money, or how many horrible thoughts were present—but I do know it was all males, and me. I sat in a sticky part of the floor, where I could see the entrance, and clutched onto myself. As grown-man jokes, grown-man crying', grown-man hungers, grown-man worries, and grown-man fancies soared above my head, I remained still and kept my eyes down. I'd get a glimpse of one of them leering at me now and then, or hear a filthy allusion to me in their talk.

I'm not sure how I got from the card room floor to the front seat of his car. What I do recall is feeling filthy as a result of the sticky floor and the men's vulgar statements. I knew my sister wasn't going to come and clean me up this time. Panic rose to the surface of my throat. What am I doing? Why am I spending my time alone with my sister's boyfriend? Why did he bring me among those vile men? How come we can't just go to IHOP? What happened to my sister? What happened to her? I started praying.

Our next visit was the drive-in, when John wrapped his arm around me almost immediately. My body stiffened. My gaze was locked on his rifle. John pushed in closer and kissed me hard. I was nauseated and terrified, and I felt immobilised. I watched an elderly white man pull up next to us and park next to us, gazing right into John's car.

The man's expression was a mix of disgust and recognition. He saw an adult guy, John, with his round Afro, and a young kid with blond coils of hair. He saw John's light-brown skin and the powder-blue automobile. He noticed the details, and even if he didn't notice my sorrow, he could tell this was not a place a young girl would want to be. John slowly exited the drive-in and drove me home in silence.

That man's visage was burned into my memory. He's still there, locked in that dreadful period. In person, I believe he was a prayer.

After a few days in my room, the phone started ringing again, but this time I didn't answer it. I went back to acting like I was in seventh grade. I wished I could be a youngster again. At night, all the kids in my area would play chase (tag). The majority of them lived in lovely houses with two parents and sisters who didn't burden them with suicidal thoughts or put them up with pimps. I yearned to blend in on an ordinary Long Island summer night, to play and laugh around with other average kids. I only wanted to outrun my drama in a pursuit game.

We used to play in a park near the ocean that had a kind of roundabout. We'd hang out there, occasionally building a fire, doing weird voices, and singing. When I saw a car coming down the road one night, we were deep in a group game of chase, kids spread about sprinting and weaving. I recognized it right away as John's automobile. It was moving slowly, like if the driver was hunting for something or someone. Panicky, I ducked behind a house, attempting to hide from whoever was "it." I couldn't tell my buddies that I was "it" to a pimp with a pistol.

Finally, John drove away. Even though I narrowly avoided him again, my fear of males lingered for a long time. When I came home, I unplugged the phone from the wall and said good-by to my big sister for good.

Nobody could tell me what had happened. I was unable to inform my mother. I lacked genuine, intimate pals. I'd never felt like I belonged. Even if I had, how could I explain it to a youngster from a normal family that ate dinner at six o'clock, went to bed at nine thirty, and got in trouble for not brushing their teeth? They'd never be able to grasp it. Big sisters are supposed to protect you, not make you seem good. As a result, I didn't disclose or trust anyone.

But you still desire your older sister as a girl, because dandelions are still flowers when they first bloom.

Among all the visits and memories, one from my sister left the strongest impression on me.

We attempted to have tea. Tea was popular in my mother's household, although it was far from appropriate. We boiled the water in a little beat-up saucepan on an old stove in the tiny, flavourless, dismal, grime-coloured kitchen, instead of a bright, whistling kettle. We didn't have matching cups and saucers; we had mismatched cups and mugs, the kind found in the "Free" box at Long Island yard sales. The standard tea taste was English breakfast, and we each had a cup with a steeping tea bag. I had a chipped lip on a thick porcelain brown drip-glaze mug. When the phone rang, I was holding the steaming, fragrant black tea in both hands.

"Oh hello, Al," our mother replied. It had to be our father.

We were both taken aback. My father rarely contacted my mother's house, and when he did, it was almost always to chastise us. Alison and I exchanged a short glance, wondering who had done what. My mother turned to face me, and I could see they were talking about me. I shook my head "no" and mimed my refusal. Alison and I were going to have tea, perhaps even a rare light moment, when I realised I'd have to get serious when it came to dealing with our father. And who knew what Alison had done that I would have to hear about?

However, Mother did not cover for us. "Yes, she's here; please hold on," she added, holding out the phone and shaking it at me. Whatever "normal sister moment" Alison and I were attempting to create was completely shattered. I straightened my back, sighed, and picked up the phone. Then I shook it and extended the cord to Alison, motioning for her to grab it.

"Nooooo, you take it," she replied. For a few moments, we engaged in a ridiculous game of who would bear the responsibility of talking to Father. It was nearly enjoyable.

Finally, I placed the receiver against my ear. "Good day, Father. "I'm fine," I responded, restraining myself from laughing. My sister began gesticulating frantically, shaking her head and slashing her fingers over her throat as I went through the mechanical pleasantries of the conversation, signalling for me not to reveal her presence. I made stupid looks back at her, doing everything I could not to giggle as I tried to keep on the conversation with our father. My sister could be quite dramatic, and I thought her especially amusing at the time. I thought we were having fun. "Guess what-Alison is here!" I remarked when I realised it was her turn to try to talk seriously to our father as I tried to make her laugh. "Would you like to talk to her?" I indicated for her to accept the phone, laughing.

But she didn't seem to notice me. She was looking down at her still-steaming tea mug, and when she lifted her gaze, her eyes were frenzied, with no sign of their prior fun. Before I knew what was going on, she shrieked "No!" and dumped the boiling-hot tea on me.

The next thing I remember is being stripped down to my waist while a doctor used enormous tweezers to remove the remaining remains of my white-and-turquoise diagonal-striped top that had become trapped in the flesh of my shoulder. Because part of the fibres in my shirt had begun to merge with my flesh, the doctor had to cut it off with an instrument. (I fucking adored that top-it was one of the few cute pieces I had, and it was now plastered to my back.)

Third-degree burns littered my back. I couldn't recognize it as mine because it had turned various hues of maroon from my sister's intense scorching. I had blacked out from the horrifying bodily experience. My back was numb after that and couldn't be touched without agonising pain. It took years for me to accept a simple pat on the back because the majority of my skin needed to entirely rejuvenate and mend itself.

The most serious injury, however, was caused by emotional anguish. Feelings are not like skin in that new cells do not appear to replace old ones. Those scars go unnoticed, unacknowledged, and unaddressed. My big sister's burn, not the tea, caused truly lasting damage to me. Her arson was intentional; she torched both my back and my trust. Any glimmer of hope I'd had of having a big sister had vanished by that time.

My sister was clearly injured. She is both the brightest and the most broken person I have ever met. I'll never understand what injured her so badly that she hurt so many others in retaliation, but she was her own most permanently damaged victim, in my opinion. From my perspective, she opted to live permanently in "Victimland." Her life's promise was squandered in a tragic succession of bad deals, rather than being redeemed via the laborious, life-long effort of healing and rebuilding oneself.

Alison has burned me numerous times and in numerous ways. I've tried several times to be her fire department, financing therapies and paying for stints at high-end rehab facilities. Even with abundant resources, there is no way to save someone who is unaware that they are on fire. My sister's scars are more than simply a remembrance; they are teachings. They've taught me that our worlds are much too different to ever collide, hers of fire and mine of light.

I always hoped and wanted Alison to improve so that we could improve. I believe she was terribly emotionally abused and had to vent her frustrations on someone. She chose me. My sister and brother have both thrown me on the chopping board over the years, selling lies to any gossip magazine or trashy website that would purchase or listen. They have been harassing me for decades. But when I was twelve, my sister drugged me with Valium, offered me a pinky nail full of cocaine, burned me to the third degree, and tried to sell me to a pimp. All of that trauma froze something in me. That's why I frequently say, "I'm eternally twelve." I'm still battling with that period.

Detangled and Swept Away

The sun shines down on me like a spotlight in the photo, and the hot dog I'm holding has a big, joyous bite ripped out of it. My hair has gold highlights, raw sienna, wheat blond, and sweet lemon highlights that are highlighted by the sun. Soft, thick waves of it are blowing away from my face in stages, with a few ringlets sweeping up off my shoulders. My glans is soft, with a hint of seriousness at the corners of my eyes.

This is one of my favourite childhood photos. In it, I appear to be an average first-grader on summer vacation. I appear to be the property of someone who knows how to look after me. I appear to be properly taken care of. However, I was not.

My youth was plagued by neglect. My mother didn't know how to nourish or keep many aspects of my personality, but the most clear, symbolic, and noticeable was my hair.

My hair was not attached to anyone. My hair was not done by anyone. Nobody knew how to do it. My mother's house didn't have a conditioner (or "cream rinse," as it was known back then). There were no pomades, combs with large teeth, or brushes with stiff bristles. There was no Sunday routine of getting my hair cleaned and braided, and certainly no scalp lubrication. In my hair, there was no order. I never felt the cleanliness or security that came with having my hair done.

As a result, my hair was frequently matted and tangled. And no one could completely comprehend the embarrassment of being a nonwhite small girl with unkempt hair. I didn't have the words for it, but I bore the weight of how it felt. My neglected hair was a warning sign that I was different from all the other little white girls—and little Black girls as well. My wild, jumbled, and deformed curls made me feel inadequate and unworthy of proper attention.

There was no way you were going to the salon, dahling. My mother never went to a salon, as far as I recall. She was a firm believer in the bohemian, no-fuss beauty concept of the 1950s and 1960s. A full beat face for her was eyeliner—a little cat wing, if she was feeling fancy-a swirl of mascara, a touch of blush, a lip, and voilà! Face is flawless. Her hair looked great up or down. Even if she had imagined she could afford professional grooming services, neither she nor I could. Furthermore, there were no salons in that section of Long Island that could understand the paradoxes of my tendrils, the sheer intricacies of my hair's needs. There were no mixed-texture professionals at the time, nor were there any specialised products. I was caught between an Afro Sheen and a Breck Girl world.

My mother and TV advertising were the two constant symbols of feminine beauty I observed on a daily basis. I adored and coveted my mother's long, luxuriant hair for its black, smooth perfection. The difference between my mother's hair and mine when she woke up in the morning was stark. She'd shake her head, and her thick, straight hair would cascade down like a yard of heavy silk crepe, hanging across her shoulders in an elegant pool. I, on the other hand, had smashed-down, fuzzy, sweaty clumps busting all over my head in a symphony of knots, waves, and curls.

Then there was the hair I saw on TV, the glorious, sunshine-filled, slow-motion-blowing-in-the-wind-while-running-barefoot-through-flower-fields hair. Those commercials, especially the ones for Clairol Herbal Essence shampoo, captivated me. It was almost as if Eve herself were in the Garden of Eden, bottling the thick, emerald-green nectar composed of earthly delights like herbs and wildflowers. I was certain that this shampoo would give me the magnificent hair seen in the commercial, blown by winds of angels' wings. I was desperate for some shampoo. I wished I had that lovely, blowing hair. (I'm still obsessed with blowing hair because of those advertisements, Olivia Newton-John, and the Boss, Diana Ross, as demonstrated by the wind machines used in practically every photo shoot of me ever.)

I was young and culturally isolated, and I had no idea how to handle my hair, let alone the guilt it caused me. I often wonder if my mother saw the carelessness that my hair revealed. Was she too engrossed with her own responsibilities to notice? Could she not feel the nasty tangles in my head's dryness and lumps and bumps? Why couldn't she just sit me down for two hours and brush my hair like Marcia

Brady did on The Brady Bunch? Maybe she felt I looked free, like an attractive flower child, in her bohemian, sixties-loving worldview. Maybe she didn't realise I was dirty.

It's complicated having one Black and one white parent, but being a little girl with a white mother who is largely shut off from other Black women and girls may be terribly lonely. I also have no multiracial role models or references. I can see why my mother didn't know how to handle my hair. My hair was primarily regular, silky curls when I was a baby. It became more sophisticated as I grew older, with various textures appearing apparently out of nowhere. She had no idea what was going on. She was perplexed and began cutting awful bangs in my hair at random (thinking bangs would behave in multiracial hair is daring).

It was a calamity, and I felt powerless to stop it. At seven years old, I honestly believed that if mother merely washed my hair with Herbal Essence, a hair fairy would appear at night and I would wake up with poof! I'd have flawless hair like my mom or the commercial females.

It took me 500 hours of beauty school training to realise that even Marcia Brady's hair wouldn't fly out with recklessness with just shampoo. Dahling, it needs a team of pros, products, and production-conditioners galore, diffusers, precision cuts, special combs, clip-ins, cameras, and, of course, wind machines. A lot of effort is required to obtain easy hair.

What I really needed was a Black woman or someone with culture, cream, and a comb! Even so, it wasn't that straightforward.

One time my father's half sisters staged an intervention of sorts, determined to "do something about that chile's hair." It was going to be an event. My father took me to my grandfather and Nana Ruby's house in Queens while I was in second grade.

I utilised humour to cope, disarm, and defend myself. I also utilised it to express myself when I was powerless. It was a tool I began sharpening early on and still use frequently now. I overheard Alison, seated up front, grumbling to him about how I was adopting my mother's idiosyncrasies and oddities (particularly those associated with white privilege) in the backseat of the car on the long drive to visit my father's family. I guess she assumed I was out in public "passing" with our white mother (as if a youngster could tell the difference).

And then, as if I weren't there, she launched into a rant. I kept staring blankly out the window at the run-down communities we'd passed through on our way from Long Island to Jamaica, Queens. It got to the point where I couldn't handle it any longer. Achieving a (I think) impressive impersonation of my mother, especially for a six-year-old, I groaned sarcastically in her characteristically slow, low, opera diva tone: "I see we're taking the scenic route!" At which Alison snapped her head toward my father with an exasperated "See?" expression on her face. He tightened his hold on the steering wheel and kept his gaze forward. I didn't break my boring stare out the window for effect. My modest mimicry did not amuse anyone. I made an attempt.

Sweet Nana Ruby was my father's father's second wife, with whom he had a slew of children, half aunties and uncles to me, who gave birth to a slew of cousins, some of whom were my age. My father had a troubled connection with his father, Bob Carey. Bob's mother was from Venezuela, and it is assumed that his father was Black—mixed with some undocumented lightening element, as he was also on the fairer half of what was then known as the "Negro spectrum."

My father hadn't spoken to his father in years until I was about six years old. He was an only child and had a different mother than my grandfather's other children, and as warm and welcome as Nana Ruby and her house were-and from what I could see, she showered my father with love-she was not his mother, and he may have felt a little out of place with them. I believe he attempted to reconcile with his father for the benefit of his own children as well as himself. He must have recognized how isolated I was, living with only my mother in an all-white neighbourhood that was growing increasingly unfriendly to me. I needed to get to know certain family members.

And I will be eternally grateful for it, because that house was a warm, bustling hub of family life. I had a great time there. My grandfather was adored by everyone in the area. He was a typical, fun-loving guy who wore crew socks with his slide sandals and had a big laugh. He had a small urban vineyard in his Queens backyard. He produced sour grapes and used them to make sweet homemade wine, which he stored in the cellar. In the tiny kitchen, Nana Ruby and my aunties constantly had something cooking-chicken, greens-but the prominent staple dish was rice and beans. I could eat several dishes of it. Pots clanging, soul music in the background, the hum of the TV, talks, chuckles, doors opening and closing, feet racing up and down the stairs: there was a cacophony of pleasant noises. It was a fun environment. People were just hanging out and were linked to one another. Being there gave me the closest feeling to having a large family, a normal family, a true family.

My favourite Bronx cousins would visit, and boy, did we play! We were a cheeky and inventive group. We used to hang out the second-story window and drop water balloon bombs on anyone going by below. Then we'd duck down and tremble in muffled hysterics, out of sight. And, of course, everything involving performance piqued my interest. My favourite was reenacting "Mrs. Wiggins" sketches from The Carol Burnett Show. Unsurprisingly, I insisted on taking centre stage. I knew her characteristic stroll was like the back of my hand. I shoved a pillow up my small booty and stuck it out like I was wearing a tight pencil skirt. I pranced around on my tippy-toes, taking little steps (maybe this is why I still walk on my toes). I'd smack imaginary gum, pretend to file my nails, and speak in my ideal ditsy, nasally voice. Early on, I concentrated on character voices.

"Oh, Mrs. Uh-Whiggins!" one of my cousins would say in a silly, skewed Swedish accent. I'd enter character and we'd dive into a full-fledged improvisation. What I enjoyed the most was the raucous laughter with my cousins. I enjoyed the sound of my own laughter as a small part of a chorus of other youngsters who were similar to me.

I may have felt a part of something inside the house with my cousins, but outside with youngsters in the neighbourhood was a different story. It's always a new story with me. Even though my cousins did not live on this predominantly Black and Hispanic Queens block, they were well-known since our grandfather was "that guy" in the area. When we were playing outside, they'd present me to the other kids as their cousin, and one of them would always respond, "She's not your cousin." She's all white."

"Yes, she is our cousin!" they would snap right back. It was never clear who my mother was, who my father was, or to whom I belonged. However, hanging out with my cousins was not as intense. I was a member of a group. They defended me because I was one of them. She is, indeed. It was that easy. And that was critical. My Black relatives were the only cousins I knew as a child. Because my mother's white relatives had shunned her, I had no possibility of having a genuine relationship with any of them as a child.

My relatives were well-dressed because their mothers were well-dressed. One auntie in particular was younger, juicier, and simply stunning. On TV, she appeared to be about to twirl down the Soul Train line. Her makeup was always flawless, and her lips were as glossy as glass. She wore funky-chic outfits, and her hair was constantly in some fantastic sleek, snatched-back style, so she could show off her face. She was always stylish, sexy, and coordinated, almost as great as Thelma on Good Times (but a touch fatter). This sassy auntie sold makeup at the department store counter—that sounded fantastic to me. She once gave my favourite girl cousin and me a mock facial examination. As she was examining our little faces, she told Cee Cee, "Your lips are good." Then she turned to me with a puzzled look and paused. What's wrong with my face, I wondered, worried. Me?

"Mariah, your lips aren't full enough," she sighed.

I had no idea why they weren't full enough, but I took her explanation as fact. A few years later, I was approximately twelve years old and hanging out with a white girlfriend at a Long Island department store where one of the counters was offering free makeup demos. My companion was a beauty by local standards, with enormous blue eyes, a narrow nose, and very thin lips. I was probably dressed haphazardly, and who knows what my hair was doing that day. We sat down to have our faces done, clearly looking our age. Maybe the saleswoman thought we had enough money to buy makeup, or she was bored, or she simply felt sorry for us. In any event, she started the process.

As my auntie had done, she studied the contours and angles of both of our faces and reported to me, "Your lips are too full on top." Wait, I thought. I was aware that my top lip was thin-but not as thin as my white acquaintance, whose lip size was the "standard" at the time. "Actually, I really want my lips to be bigger," I wanted to remark, as I had done since the day of my auntie's appraisal, but I held my tongue. As a result, as a girl, I had two polar different expert assessments about my lips: they were too full for a white beauty standard and not full enough for a Black beauty standard. Who could I believe? It was as if my complexes were complexes. And there was no one to tell me, "Mariah, you are good." Period.

And today we live in a world where white and black women fill their buttocks and lips like water balloons. I suppose I should have gotten my lips injected years ago, but it's too late now. Why bother when everyone knows what my true lips look like? Why would I do that now, dahling, when I can merely highlight them with lip liner?

But I'm getting ahead of myself. When I was seven years old, it was time for my cousins' big day at Grandpa and Nana Ruby's house. My aunts had decided it was time to assemble me. They summoned me up from Nana Ruby's bedroom, where some of them had gathered. My cousins and I went upstairs to the master bedroom, which was directly across from the bathroom. I spent many moments exploring that little bathroom, fascinated with all the greasings and slatherings it contained. There were endless creams and lotions for the skin, and dressings and pomades for the hair. Imagine: skin lotion and hair grease! In this bathroom every cabinet and free space was filled with mysterious potions and products.

I rarely went into the master bedroom, but it, too, was small, cramped, and comforting. It was humid and smelled like a hot candy store. A large bed, covered with a shiny, quilted white-and-maroon paisley bedspread, with ruffles at the hem, took up most of the room. There was a full-length mirror attached to the back of the door and a low dresser drawer on which my aunties had everything laid out. There was a hot plate cranking. Upon its sizzling surface was some foreign object that resembled a garden tool, with a dark wooden handle like a hammer, with teeth. Though the metal part was blackened, traces of its original gold colour could be seen underneath. This mysterious hammer-fork thing sat menacingly on the plate's surface, getting hotter and hotter. As I crossed the threshold into the bedroom, I felt as though I had entered an alternate universe, a secret chamber-one of Black-girl beauty.

My aunts motioned for me to sit on the side of the bed. I didn't know what kind of ritual was ahead, but I sure was excited. As I settled in on the edge of the bed, feet dangling off the side, I could feel many hands exploring the wild garden of knots, curls, and straight bits that made up my head of hair. My heart was racing. I felt like a long-lost princess sitting in her chambers, hoping this could be it—the moment of coronation, when my hair would finally get done and I would be transformed, presented to the world with newfound power and grace.

Finally, I thought, maybe my hair would fit in. Maybe it would fall into sleek and shiny ringlets, and I would look like my cute Black girl cousins and friends who gathered in Queens. Or maybe it would lie down flat and bone straight like the hair of the little white girls I grew up among on Long Island. Either way, I was just thrilled that my hair would at last be cared for by someone who knew what to do.

The straining and separating began at the back of my head, with a little pain from knots being undone. The next sensation I had was one I'll never forget. There was a heavy tugging and burning sensation at my neck, followed by a frightening scorching and sizzling sound and an unknown and nasty odour, similar to a dirty stuffed animal set on fire. A subtle worry began to flow through the room, along with heavy smoke. I couldn't understand much of what was said, but I did hear "Oh shit!" and "Stop, stop!" multiple times. And suddenly it came to a halt. Abruptly. The thrill, ritual, and fixing all came to a halt. I remained immobile and silent, a small patch of burning hair at the nape of my neck remaining.

My aunts apologised profusely. "Sorry, baby, the hot comb is too strong for your hair," my aunts said. That's all there was to it, sweetie. That day, there would be no rites of passage into Black-girl hair society. I didn't emerge as a pretty little girl fit for Harlem, Queens, or Long Island. I was still a mischievous little misfit with a disobedient crown on her head, but this time I had a patch of rough, scorched, uneven (and noticeably shorter) hair in the back. I was far from finished.

My mother, brother, and I would occasionally drive to Jones Beach as a family. (Being close to the shore was one of the few advantages of being stranded on Long Island.) The three of us kids, along with one of my brother's friends, packed into my mother's clunker on wheels and drove to the beach one summer morning. The sky was clear and brilliant, and you could see the ocean. It was a beautiful day for a trip to the beach. My mother was driving in a light-blue cotton summer caftan with delicate green stripes. My mother's bell sleeves swung slightly in the breeze as the windows were rolled down to simulate a convertible. Her typical huge sunglasses were on, and her hair was loose as usual. My shirtless brother sat next to her, his large, fluffy Afro gently swinging.

I sat silently in the backseat next to my brother's friend, gazing out the open window and letting the warm, salty air wash over my face. I was trying not to show it, but I had a huge crush on this teen-star-looking boy. His hair was strawberry blond with natural highlights, styled in delicate, feathery layers, and parted down the middle. Every dreamy strand was perfectly placed. We were all content in the car, which was unusual for us.

But gradually, I became aware that my hair was moving. But it wasn't caused by the wind. Instead, it came from what appeared to be fingers. My hair was a wild, tangled thicket, and fingers were rummaging through it. I didn't dare to move or say anything. But the boy was delicately picking at my hair! He worked surgically on the tiny, tighter, matted portions at the ends with the large black plastic comb he had in his back pocket. He was running his comb through his field of flawless golden strands on my tousled head! He drew the comb in little parts from scalp to end. Each part would float a little as it was freed from the weight of its earlier twisted confinement.

He removed all the knots and confusion from my hair during the ride, without a single word passed between us. My hair was no longer a bother by the time we got to the beach. It had been set free. I went straight to the water-oh, how I love the ocean, a gift from my mother-and as I ran, I could feel my hair for the first time, buoyant and blowing in the wind. Hallelujah! My hair was literally blowing in the wind, just like in the advertisements!

I jumped into the first wave that came my way and rode it back to land. When I stood up and stroked my hair, it wasn't the haphazard combination of textures that I was used to. Instead, I brushed against tidy, coily, elongated curls! My hair felt nice for the first time. I felt lovely. I felt soft and light, like if the shame I'd been carrying had been drained from me.

A sudden wall of waves erupted, smashing down, pounding on my back as I stood in waist-deep water, basking in the increased confidence provided by my released curls. My feet were swept up and over my head from the sandy floor. My little body was flung around like a rag doll in the powerful waves that had suddenly risen. I had no feeling of balance or orientation, but I knew I was being dragged down, falling in surging, black water mixed with frothy white foam and grit that smashed against my body like sandpaper boxing gloves. Even if I knew which way was up and how to get there, I knew I wouldn't be able to overcome the strong currents, so I relaxed my body and went with it. I bowed out.

The ocean decided to return me to the land by what I consider to be God's grace. I was winded and salty as I lay unmoving on the coarse, wet sand. When I realised I was still alive, I got up and went to find my mother. I noticed her and my brother lying on an olive blanket in the distance, shades on, sunning casually. Oblivious. I let out a powerful shriek that escalated into uncontrollable wailing, ultimately drawing my mother's attention. Yet another close call with death.

Someone took me up to the boardwalk, to the hot dog vendor, to settle my frazzled seven-year-old nerves. My hair was a mess, but I wasn't. It remained in wavy ringlets. I had perfected my beach hair. I almost died that day, but my hair was done.

A Girl's Best Friend

I felt admiration and identification from the moment I saw her. I admired her. She was a living doll, but not a baby or a Barbie; despite the fact that she was a real, elegant, grown-up woman, she appeared pristine and flawless, as if made of delicate lacquered porcelain. I'd never seen someone like her before-such a dazzling, glamorous, vulnerable, and powerful human. She possessed magical abilities. I stood there, captivated and motionless, in front of the bright screen where she lived.

One evening, I was wandering aimlessly down the corridor in one of the various houses where we lived. I walked inside my mother's dark small bedroom as I passed by. I'm not sure if I saw or heard her first, but I know something drew me inside that room. The only light in the room came from the washed-out colours of the old TV facing the bed, where my mother lay in silhouette, watching a special about Marilyn Monroe's life and death.

I carefully opened the bedroom door, entering the legendary scene from Gentlemen Prefer Blondes in which Marilyn sings "Diamonds Are a Girl's Best Friend." She was the most stunning woman I had ever seen.

Her energy was that of a fairy, but she appeared like a goddess, dressed in a beautiful electric-pink silk gown and matching opera gloves, with diamonds of all sizes falling from her ears and wrapping around her neck and wrists. Her only exposed skin was her face, shoulders, and arms down to the elbow, yet I recall her flesh being thick and creamy, gleaming like handmade ice cream. Her hair had lightened a few tones, gleaming like finely spun gold. She had round, curved hips, a small, pinched waist, proud, purposeful breasts, and arms that stretched wide and gripped close. She was poised, almost like a dancer, yet her feet didn't move. Instead, throngs of people danced about her, fawning and fanning her, kneeling and bowing to her, and carrying her above their heads like Cleopatra. Maybe she was a queen, I reasoned. The movie industry's dazzling queen.

I'd never heard of Marilyn Monroe until that moment. But I was instantly sucked in. Perhaps not usual third-grade fodder, but my childhood was anything but average. My mother enthusiastically encouraged my interest in Marilyn Monroe. Most girls my age had posters of Holly Hobbie-the frontier rag doll with freckles and blond yarn braids in a strawberry-print bonnet-on their walls, but I had a poster of Marilyn Monroe dressed as a sensuous showgirl, complete with a black beaded bustier, fishnets, and black patent-leather pumps. I looked up at Marilyn before going to bed and first thing in the morning.

My mother later got me Norman Mailer's Marilyn: A Biography. I read voraciously, despite the fact that I was far too young for the subject. I studied the large, glossy images of her, noting her various moods and appearances. She was a shape-shifter, seeming astonishingly gorgeous and glamorous in some images and shattered and about to vanish in others. Her hairstyles changed as well: pin curls, pigtails, sweeping updos, and bobs with deep-diving waves. I even noticed wild curls and familiar fuzz beneath her hair's beautiful, nearly white-blonde flow. Something about her physically, something about her body type, didn't read as typically Caucasian to me. She was not just curvy, but she also possessed a distinct sensuality that bordered on soulfulness.

I read a lot about Marilyn, including conspiracy theories concerning her death and upbringing. The more I read about her, the more I felt connected to her and realised why I was drawn to her. She had a tough childhood, going from foster family to foster home. That was similar to my experience: being uprooted and unprotected, and feeling like an outsider. I was intimately familiar with her challenges with poverty and family. Finally, what I admired about Marilyn was her capacity to emerge from nowhere—to belong to no one—and become a big symbol. That piqued my interest. That was something I believed in.

Marilyn is said to have been my mother's inspiration for my name. The initial four letters of the word are the same: M-A-R-I. My father, on the other hand, said that my name is derived from the Black Maria/Mariah, the infamous police van used to transport people to prison in the United Kingdom. I was also named after a popular 1950s show tune, "They Call the Wind Maria," from Paint Your Wagon, a Broadway musical about the California Gold Rush. (Both sources employ a soft pronunciation with a rye sound on the second syllable.) Maybe it's a mix of the three: a 1950s starlet, a show tune, and a paddy van.

Whatever the origin, I didn't enjoy my name when I was younger. Nobody else had it, which isn't cool when you're a kid. I've always wanted a common name like Jennifer or Heather. My name wasn't on any attractive stickers, key chains, or small licence plates. The worst part was that almost no one could pronounce it. I feared seeing a substitute instructor because I knew roll call would be a Maria/Maya disaster. I didn't meet another Mariah until I was approximately eighteen years old; she was a nice Black girl, and we laughed over our early mispronunciations. I had no idea that only a few years later, many parents would name their children Mariah after me.

The Marilyn Monroe connection resonates the most with me of all the alleged influences for my name-self-created and controlled, confident and vulnerable, womanly and infantile, glamorous and humble, revered and alone. Marilyn is a source of inspiration for me, which I much needed.

I urgently wanted to befriend a group of gorgeous, predominantly Irish ladies when I was in eighth grade. Most of these girls were regarded as the epitome of physical perfection in that town at the time: creamy skin, silky hair, and blue eyes. "Blue eyes rule!" they used to chant. These were not lovely ladies.

And I felt completely inadequate in their presence. My skin was filthy and my hair was unruly in comparison to them (and in eighth grade, comparison is the only technique of measuring). They called me Fozzie Bear (from the Muppets) because of my unruly hair, and no matter how hard I tried, I could never get it to look like theirs, and my eyes were definitely and undeniably unblue. (I adored my dark eyes, but I never spoke up during their strange chant.) Clearly, I stood out in their company, but they allowed me to hang out with them. Perhaps it was because I was the class clown, always ready to crack a joke or snap at someone and make the entire class laugh. Even if I was merely there to entertain, I was delighted to put on a show.

The girl in that group who was my closest buddy (and I use the term loosely) was also the most beautiful. I suppose she's now referred to as a "frenemy." I'd tell her I was interested in a boy at school, and knowing full well that I never acted on any of my crushes, she'd go after him and nearly always win. I feel she did this to humiliate me and demonstrate her dominance. But she didn't know that I never pursued boys because I didn't want to face the inevitable humiliation once they discovered that half of me was Black and all of me was impoverished. She also had no idea that I didn't want to become involved with some silly boy and ruin my aspirations, or, worse, become pregnant like my sister. She had no idea who I was. None of them succeeded.

However, some of the girls' parents knew my mother. They felt a certain amount of respect for her since she was Irish and a professional opera singer-and opera was a classy thing to do. Adult drama differs from teen drama, however the two frequently interact. It was discovered that the beautiful girl's Irish father was violently beating her mother. My mother, who can be quite righteous when she wants to, decided to write him a letter. I'm very sure she revealed in that letter that she had been married to a Black guy and that he was the father of her children (of course, I didn't learn about the letter until much later).

As I previously stated, these were not pleasant females, but I was finally asked to a sleepover in Southampton with some of them, including the prettiest one. Barbara, one of them, was a wealthy aunt with a luxurious home near the ocean. Southampton, fancy-schmancy? What about a sleepover with the popular girls? Of course, I was eager to go. We jumped into one of their large cars and drove the two hours along Long Island's stunning Atlantic coast to the small community where the wealthy "summer." (For me, summer was a season, not a verb.)

The house was spacious, light, and well-organised. It even featured an all-white area that no one could enter. When we arrived, I was so caught up in comparing and yearning that I hadn't spotted the girls gathering in a huddle beside a door.

"Come on, Mariah," they said to me. Let's return here."

Without a doubt, I followed. They escorted me to what I assumed was a playroom or a den (I'd heard wealthy people had dens). It was a smaller room in the back of the home, possibly a guest room. One of them clicked the door shut, and the mood quickly became heavy. I assumed they'd sneaked in some alcohol or something. There was, however, no thrill, no wicked, female energy. Instead, every single girl was staring at me. Into the heavy stillness, the beautiful girl's sister spat out her horrible secret for all to hear: "You're a nigger!"

When I understood she was referring to me, my head began to spin. I saw you pointing at me. It was my shame, my secret. I was paralyzed.

The rest swiftly followed suit. "You're a nigger!" exclaimed everyone. They all chanted in unison, "You're a nigger!" over and over. I believed it would go on forever.

The vitriol and hatred with which these females shouted this new version of their normal chant literally took me out of my body. I had no notion how to deal with what was happening. They were all working against me. It was all planned. They duped me into thinking they liked me. They drew me away from home for hours. They had me isolated. They had me entrapped. Then they turned on me. I burst into violent tears. I was disoriented and afraid, and I hoped that if I just hung on and cried, a grown-up would come and stop the assault. But no one showed up.

I eventually heard another crying voice among the crowd.

"Why are you doing this?" inquired the small, bold voice. She was the eldest blond.

The unattractive sister of the prettiest said, "Because she is a nigger."

I don't recall anything else from that day. I have no recollection of the ride home. I don't recall informing my mother when I returned. How can you explain to your all-white mother that your all-white "friends" led you into their large all-white house in all-white Southampton, past an untouchable all-white chamber, only to corner you and label you the dirtiest thing in their all-white world? Nigger.

I was also concerned that my mother would cause a public uproar, making life at school much more difficult for me. I have no language or coping abilities to deal with any of this. It was not the first time I had been humiliated by my classmates. On the school bus, I'd been singled out and spit on. I'd been into physical altercations. My tongue was sharp, and I could be a real wiseass, so I would often clap back. I've even started fights on occasion. But I had no defence for this. I was not only outnumbered and isolated, but I had also been betrayed.

This was no ordinary mean-girl brawl in the playground. It was a cunning and severe premeditated assault carried out by girls I called my friends. I never mentioned it. I stuffed it in there. I had to figure out how to go through those females, that place, my family, and my suffering.

"Mariah only has three shirts and she puts them in rotation!"

The harsh comments exploded like a stink bomb into the bustling bustle of my seventh-grade hallway's in-between-class traffic. The pattering of feet, the clanging of lockers, the chirping of small conversation, and the little chuckles merged into one enormous laughing monster formed of students, sitting in the centre of the corridor and pointing at me. My gut collapsed and my face caught fire. I thought I was going to puke on the tile floor.

Middle school is a rough environment, and I was rather skilled with my own sharp tongue. Many children had to endure cruel or "funny" labels given to them by their peers because of how they appear or some embarrassing event, but being taunted for being poor felt different.

I was gravely damaged, but I didn't show it. I didn't throw up in front of everyone. Nobody got the satisfaction of seeing me weakened. I remained emotionless while I waited for the monster to vanish, since traffic had to restart and students had to get to their classes. After that, I realised there was no going back and no attempting to fit in. I'd subsist on the outside with three shirts and no friends, hoping to eventually relocate again.

In our middle-class neighbourhood, I was quite self-conscious about living in a little decaying house with a shabby wardrobe; yet, by the time I started high school, I had learned some new survival skills. I didn't have any say over where I resided at the time, but I could choose what I wore. One of the few benefits of moving so frequently was that I always had a new group of youngsters to try to fit in with. I managed to gather a few girlfriends and persuade them that we could start a fashion trading system in which we'd exchange our trendiest clothes with one another and coordinate them differently. This gave the impression that I had a larger and more current wardrobe than I could possibly afford.

The coolest item I possessed was an oversized red wool and black leather varsity jacket with AVIREX written across the back in huge letters. It was important to me to have a name-brand item, so I made sure I had a trademark piece that could be dressed up or down. To fit in with the other Long Island females, I tried my hardest to look like a typical cute suburban teen.

I was "going out" with the biggest and scariest male in town by the ninth grade. He stood six feet five inches tall and had biceps that were larger than both of my thighs. He was in his early twenties, had a car, and no one bothered him. That was the main reason I was with him. He was a shield, a force field. My former boyfriend was explosive; we even got into a physical fight in front of a bunch of girls who stood around and watched. He stalked and harassed me after we broke up—a true charmer. Mr. Six Foot Five caught him verbally assaulting me before lifting him off the ground and tossing him over five parked cars-pow! Aside from his raw power, he was actually quite chill. However, high school can be dangerous, especially for an outsider like me, so having the hardest guy in town as my guy was beneficial at the time.

I never understood a group of gals who were into a sixties tie-dyed Grateful Dead feel. It was the late 1980s, and the street fashion was so new that I had no idea what they were doing. Why were they going for such an odd throwback look? They were also aggressive and hard, not hippies, Dead Heads, or peaceniks. I called them the "Peace People" since I was a clever aleck. They were furious when they found out I was making fun of them. Rumours began to circulate that I was about to get my ass kicked. But Mr. Six Foot Five was legendary; everyone feared him, so getting at me wasn't that easy.

After finishing my morning habit of going to the Bagel Station for a bagel with bacon and cheese and coffee, I was strolling down the walkway to "the patio" to drink my coffee and smoke a Newport before homeroom. The patio was a big brick area outside the school cafeteria where students would hang out, smoke, and pose. Several hundred yards before I got there, a semicircle of around a dozen white girls closed in on me, all pumped up to fight.

They were all screaming at the same time, and the toughest of them all broke free from the pack and ran at me. I was terrified but tried hard not to show it. The bagel in my stomach had transformed into rocket fuel and was exploding in my stomach, and my mind was racing with ideas on how to defuse or divert the situation, because I was not going to fight. I had a rough exterior and a wiseass tongue, but I never wanted to fight anyone. I used my wits to survive (and, except for one boy, I was the quickest runner in the school). The mob mentality of the crowd had come near enough to singe the hairs on my arms. I needed to say something, so I opened my mouth and started yelling-I'm not sure what. What I'll never forget is watching their arrogance fade into timidity as they slowly slid backward and dispersed. I believed I had truly told them off for a split second, but then I felt a powerful spirit behind me. When I turned back, there was a giant gorgeous wall of every style, size, and shade of every Black female I knew in school, appearing like a fly-girl adolescent version of a Black Panther protest. "Oh, we've got your back," one of them said, and that was the end of the conversation.

There was no dispute about "how Black" I was or if I "looked white"-those fierce girls simply told me that if it came down to it, they were going to hold me down.

Years later, following the publication of "Vision of Love," I was everywhere on radio and television. My mother was still on Long Island, so I asked if we might go by the house where the most beautiful girl and her sisters lived. I pulled over, got out, and just stared at the humble edifice, a symbol of everything I had endured. My mother followed, covered in a fur coat I'd given her. The father of the family (the one who had beaten the mother) arrived at the door and exclaimed, "Aw, look, Pat's gone Hollywood!" in his thick, twangy Long Island accent. The remainder of the family made their way out of the house. The most beautiful one was taken aback. She couldn't believe what had occurred.

The mutt-mulatto babe who lived in the run-down shack down the street had become a celebrity.

"You're a loser!" said the brother.

That family, that house, that town, that time, that day-it all seemed so insignificant to me. It was nothing in the middle of nowhere, and I had made it out.

"Mariah, I'm so happy for you; I'm so happy for you!" the blond girl exclaimed as I turned to get back in the car. And she grew into the most beautiful of the sisters.

PART II: SING. SING.

A Prelude to Sing Sing

Even now, it's difficult to articulate how I existed in my connection with Tommy Mottola. It's not that there are no words; they just get caught travelling up from my core or disappear into the thicket of my anxiousness. Tommy's intensity was tremendous, if not overpowering; it was an entire atmosphere for me. I could feel the air change and my breath shorten even before he entered the room. He washed over me like fog. His presence was suffocating and dense. He was unavoidable, like dampness.

I never felt like I could breathe freely and totally as myself when I was with him. His authority was all-encompassing, and it brought with it an unfathomable sense of uneasiness. I was walking on eggshells at the start of our time together. Then it became a nail bed, and then a minefield. I never knew when or what would set him off, and the dread was constant. In the eight years we were together, I can't remember a single ten-minute period when I felt at ease-or at all. I could feel his hands choking me off from my essence. I was disintegrating in stages.

He seemed to be cutting off my circulation, isolating me from my friends and what little "family" I had. I couldn't communicate with anyone who wasn't under Tommy's authority. I couldn't go anywhere or do anything with anyone. In my own home, I couldn't move about freely.

Many evenings, I would lie on my side of our huge bed, beneath which I kept my purse stocked with supplies in case I needed to flee quickly-my "to go" bag. I had to wait for him to nod off. I would gently inch my way to the edge of the bed, keeping my gaze fixed on him, and surgically roll my hips and swing my legs to the floor. I'd tiptoe backward toward the entrance, which looked a whole city block away, never breaking my stare. I'd back out of the door with caution. It felt like such a win when I finally got out of the room! I'd silently creep down the huge dark-wood staircase like a burglar stealing a moment's solitude, then make my way to somewhere in the mansion. Often, all I wanted to do was walk to the kitchen for a snack or sit at the table and scribble some lyrics. But every time, just as I was beginning to relax into the quiet darkness and find my breath-Beep! Beep! The intercom would ring.

I'd spring up, and the words "Whatcha doin'?" would crackle over the speaker, causing me to gulp and lose my own air once more. Every step I took, every place I went, was being watched minute by minute, day by day, year by year.

It seemed as if I were being crushed to death. Everything he didn't feel he could produce or control was being strangled. I made the fun and free girl in my films so I could watch a version of myself come to life, so I could live vicariously through her-the girl I pretended to be, the person I wanted was me. My videos would serve as proof that I existed.

I was living my dream but was unable to leave my home. I was held captive in that relationship, lonely and trapped. Captivity and control can take many forms, but the goal is always the same: to weaken the captive's will, remove any sense of self-worth, and erase the person's recollection of their own soul. I'm still not sure how much of me was permanently damaged or arrested, including, among other things, my capacity to properly trust people or entirely rest. But, happily, I was able to smuggle myself out gradually through the lyrics of my songs. What I couldn't say was expressed via song. I can't forget, no matter how hard I try. I am sometimes troubled by nightmares or glimpses of suffocation without warning. I still feel the burden from time to time. I occasionally run out of air.

Alone in Love

I had my first professional recording session while I was in seventh school. I sang backup vocals on a few original songs, including a rendition of Peabo Bryson's famous R&B ballad "Feel the Fire," which he wrote and recorded. The session took place in a small home studio, but it was a real job for which I was paid real money. It was also during this time that I began to learn how to produce nuances and textures in vocal compositions, as well as how to use my voice to build layers like a painter. This is where my love affair with the studio began. This was a watershed moment in my journey, my will to succeed.

One session gig led to another. I felt like a giant fish in a puddle. The Long Island music scene was limited, and word of mouth was the primary way of promotion. I was writing songs and recording background vocals and jingles for local businesses by the age of fourteen or fifteen. I was performing background vocals for these young Wayne's World sort of guys on a regular basis. They were into crazy, loud guitar riffs and such, whereas I was enamoured with contemporary urban radio, which was largely R&B, hip-hop, and dance music. I was addicted to the radio. Despite the fact that our tastes were plainly extremely different, I like the job. I was recording demos for songs and advertisements and learning how to change my voice to whatever task was at hand. My natural habitat was the studio. When I was there, I felt weightless, as if I were in the ocean, and all my external troubles faded away. I concentrated solely on the music, and even if I didn't enjoy their songs, I admired the effort that went into creating them. I informed them I was a songwriter once, when we were working on one of their music mashups. I reasoned that if we could work on their corny stuff, why couldn't we work on mine?

Technically, I had been writing since I was a child. In my diary, I drew poems and song drawings. I'd have a moment of lightness in the little, dim living room, sitting on the wooden piano stool at my mother's amazingly well-kept brown upright Yamaha piano, whether I was alone in the house or my mother was asleep. I'd lean my diary against the music shelf, my feet dangling. I'd hum a song and look for the keys that were closest to my voice. Then, almost whisperingly, I'd sing a few words along with the melody.

I had faith in the music I was hearing in my head. I assumed it was similar to popular songs I heard on the radio. My songs didn't try to imitate the style or sound of what I heard; instead, I was always looking for the appropriate sound, one that felt like me. And I was confident that my voice would blend in with, if not outperform, what was playing on the radio. That was something I truly believed. I was aware that what I was hearing was advanced for my age, but I was fortunate to be working with two guys who were really collaborative and receptive to working with such a young and female artist. So, in their mother's house, in a sad little slapped-together studio, I wrote and produced one of my favourite demos, "To Begin" (I still love it, but unhappily, it's among the many lost cassettes of tiny Mariah). I was convinced that I had a good tune.

"Why are we listening to this little kid?" they wondered. To be honest, I don't think they grasped the culture, genres, and tones I was working with. They were strange tiny garage-band hippie-type men. I was a small kid, but I also recognized where the pulse of the society was—and they weren't near it. Working with them forced me to be disciplined. But I had outgrown them by the time I was fifteen.

One of my first regular gigs was with these two shady guys doing demos. They liked my music because it had that young-girl character that was fashionable at the time, thanks in large part to Madonna's success. But I was a young girl, and my vocals could naturally reach that high pitch range. I could imitate Madonna's famed studio method, but just with my voice.

I auditioned by singing one of their songs, and they hired me right away. So the shady individuals started paying me to perform demos. This was the official start of my professional career—along with a never-ending string of dubious personalities. I'd ventured into the perilous zone of the "music industry." Though my path was just beginning, I would soon be introduced to the complex dynamics that female artists must deal with. Most don't make it, as I've discovered.

There were strange vibes from the start because I couldn't tell if these guys were pervy or not, but I was confident that nothing insane would happen because they both had wives who were always around. I naively imagined these ladies playing big-sister roles alongside me. They were all full-fledged adults, and I was still a child, but my age and talent produced conflict. Even though I was a tiny young teenager (my body was pretty much a straight line at that age), I threatened one of the wives. She was usually nearby, bouncing around in short shorts and exuding nasty energy. I had no idea what was going on. I was too young to understand it, and I was also there to work. Perhaps my own short shorts were unacceptable in the presence of these older men. I had no idea. I was just a kid enjoying her first taste of independence, and all I had were a few pairs of inexpensive shorts and blouses. I was fighting a battle of the short shorts and didn't even realise it.

I kept making a little money by recording song demos for the guys. But, as with the garage-band fellows, we were recording their tunes, even though I thought mine were better. I also asked if I could write some tunes for them. They initially declined. It was extremely frustrating: here I was again, performing strange, cheesy songs. Did these people not even turn on the radio? I was perplexed. Did they not realise what was popular? I paid great attention to the music on the radio, always scrutinising what was on repeat. I could tell the songs they were writing were bad. Despite the fact that I disliked the material, I sang it since it was my work and I really needed the money. But now that I'd had a taste of recording demos, I realised I needed to record my own songs as soon as possible.

Later, I struck a deal with one of the people who owned a studio: I would sing demos for him in exchange for the freedom to work on my own. I brought in one of the tunes I'd started at my mother's piano at the shack, "Alone in Love." I sat alone in a room and started making my first demonstrations. My own.

I figured out how to do it. I played around with the music. I did dance tunes, straight down the line, with a variety of sounds. I learnt how to work under duress. I was working on it in the studio. "Alone in Love" was one of my earliest demo tunes. A version of the song ended up on my first CD and is still one of my favourites.

Cherchez La Femme

Towards the conclusion of the evening, Brenda said, "I'm going to take you to this party, and you're going to meet a big record executive, Jerry Greenberg, and it's going to be great."

Yes, why not? I pondered. I was feeling confident enough in my professional abilities to allow her to take me to an industry party. I was recording sessions and had a deal with Warners in the works for one of my songs to be used in a film. I wasn't very engaged in this party. Brenda had a big heart, but she could also be a little crazy, so I had to take a lot of what she said with a grain of salt.

We were going to get ready in her house in Jersey because she had all the clothes, cosmetics, and accessories she needed from being on tour and having some money. She was supposed to come and get me from my apartment. I sat in my tight vestibule for nearly an hour, sprawled on the tile floor (there was no texting back then). Finally, she appeared, pumped up, energised, and ready to party. Her enthusiasm was contagious.

We began our evening routine in her spacious bathroom. Brenda had every type of mousse, hair spray, comb, and curler imaginable. I could easily work with what she had given her mixed Puerto Rican and Jewish ancestry. By twisting pieces of hair around the rod of a curling wand, I sought to create one long, uniform coil all around my head. I completed it with a solid bang. She let me borrow a small black dress (what else!). I had brought my own opaque black tights, but they were too small to go into her shoes. So I wore my black Vans with ribbed slouchy socks. I finished the look with my one standout piece, a high school Avirex jacket.

I really tried with my appearance, and it worked out. Brenda told me the party was to commemorate the launch of a new record company, but since I was already interested in the major labels with the big boys and big musicians, I didn't have great hopes for who would be there. The new label was the result of a collaboration between three well-known industry figures who had formed their own label, WTG Records. The letters "WTG" stood for Walter, Tommy, and Gerald. It seemed like a tire company to me; I didn't know who anyone was yet. But Brenda knew Jerry (Gerald Greenberg), who she said was a huge deal in the industry (in 1974, at thirty-two, he became Atlantic Records' youngest-ever president). When she explained this, the party became a little more interesting.

Brenda had brought me there to see a person from Atlantic Records, which explained why she wanted me to bring my demo (not that I ever went anywhere without it). When we arrived at the party, I found myself surrounded by "industry people," though I had no idea what that meant. I took in the scenery as I wandered about. A female artist was being dragged around by her handlers like a show horse. She was very blond, very lovely, very white, and very dolled up and coiffed, surrounded by a flurry of labelled people in a tight, buzzing cloud. There were blown-up photos of her all throughout the place.

We were probably intended to ooh and ahh in her presence. But I had no interest in her. I was simply wondering to myself, "Who is she, and why should I be excited?" To me, she was simply another person they were carrying about. To be honest, I was underwhelmed by the entire scene.

Brenda and I took a seat at a table. We were attempting to have fun in a room full of suits, but all I could think about was being at the studio working on tunes or anything. That was always where I wanted to be. We stood up to use the restroom, weaving our way through the mob to the stairs that led to the restrooms.

I noticed him as we jumped up the stairs.

He wasn't someone I'd ordinarily notice: he wasn't exceptionally tall or short, stylish or tacky. I'm quite sure he was dressed up. He would have been completely forgotten if it hadn't been for his eyes. Our gazes connected, and an energy surged between us, like to a faint electric shock. He had a hard look.

He peered into me rather than at me. I was a little shaken—not in a terrible way, but also not in a love-at-first-sight kind of way. I continued up the steps, this time at a slower speed, while I processed what had just occurred. The strange sensation continued to pulsate through me even after I shut the restroom door. What had occurred? I had no idea who he was, but I recognized him. I knew it wasn't from television or anything. It wasn't his face that was the problem; it was something else. I sensed his energy, and I believe he sensed mine.

Brenda was overjoyed. "Did you notice how Tommy Mottola regarded you? "I did!" she said, her eyes wide open.

"Who's Tommy Mottola?" I inquired.

"Girl." She stared at me, puzzled, with a serious expression on her face. "'Who's Tommy Mottola?'!" She began singing a well-known refrain: "Tommy Mottola lives on the road... You don't know who it is, and you've never heard that song?" My head shook. She continued to sing: "Oh, oh, oh, oh, oh cherchez, cherchez—"

It struck me. "Oh! Yes, I recognize that tune!" "Oh, oh, oh, oh, oh, oh, oh, cherchez, cherchez," I said. "Cherchez la Femme / Se Si Bon," by Dr. Buzzard's Original Savannah Band, was the song.

I told her that I used to like that song when I was a kid.

"That's Tommy from that song," Brenda replied. He's one of the biggest record producers of all time." Brenda and I went over to where they were all standing.

I stood there wondering what he wanted with me if he was such a big shot. The girls at the party were much more attractive, with professional makeup and significantly superior footwear. "Who's your friend?" Tommy asked Brenda, the most intense three words I'd ever heard.

Brenda addressed her response to Jerry. "Her name is Mariah, and she's eighteen years old." You have to hear this!" Tommy's hand abruptly stopped her off mid-extension as she moved to offer Jerry my sample cassette. He grabbed the tape, stood up, left the table, and exited the party. It was strange and perplexing. What kind of nonsense is that?

That was a significant demonstration. It had some of my favourite songs, including "All in Your Mind," "Someday," and "Alone in Love." Had Tommy just taken all that effort (and money!)? I wasn't thinking to myself, "Yay, I just gave my demo to a big-time record executive." I was more concerned with the fact that I had one additional copy of my demo. I knew Tommy was never going to listen to me, I reasoned.

According to common belief, Tommy left the party to go into his limo, where he could quickly listen to the demo. I had no idea why he had departed the party so abruptly. But once he did, I was ready to leave as well. As a result, I did.

Tommy eventually returned in search of me, obviously unable to believe what he had just heard had come from that same girl on the stairs, the innocent-looking kid in Vans and floppy socks. All those dressed-up girls in high heels were trying so hard to catch W, T, or G's attention—and T came back seeking for me.

Tommy was already the head of Sony Music, so obtaining my phone number was a piece of cake. He called and left a message on my voicemail.

Josefin and I created performance art by messing about and making up ridiculous voices on the answering machine. I'd come in from the studio at five a.m., and we'd make these bizarre messages. I was imitating her Swedish accent in the one Tommy heard: "If this is the super, we need some help here!" Flies are in our cats' tails. "There's no hot water," she exclaimed, followed by uncontrollable laughter. It was amusing to us, but it was also true. The circumstances in our apartment were deplorable. We had sticky flypaper on the ceiling and walls that our cats would brush up against. We also didn't have hot water; it was a disaster. But we were young, eager females who made a comedy out of our situation.

Tommy hung up the first time he called. But he refused to quit. He called back and left a short but serious message: "Tommy Mottola." Sony Records. CBS." He left a phone number. "Call me back."

It was impossible for me to believe. I called Brenda right away, and she confirmed that Tommy's office had called her manager, and he wanted to sign me. This was the first in a bizarre and fanciful succession of Cinderella stories that would follow in my life. But I wasn't taken off my feet, and believe me when I say Tommy Mottola was no Prince Charming.

A Family

It was the middle of July 1993, and I was on my way to Schenectady, New York, to tape an NBC Thanksgiving special. It was the first event to launch promotion for my upcoming third studio album, Music Box. The first single, "Dreamlover," would be published in a week, and the whole album would be released on August 31. Schenectady, a typical eastern New York industrial city, was mostly made up of Eastern European immigrants and Black people who had moved from the South to work in the town's cotton mill. Hillsjail is a direct shot north along the Hudson River.

The event was to be taped in Proctors Theatre, a former vaudeville venue complete with a red carpet, gold leaf everywhere, Corinthian columns, chandeliers, and Louis XV couches in the balcony promenade-the works. Even though it was a lovely, vintage theatre, it was not a venue I would have selected, nor would most twenty-somethings in the early 1990s. However, I made few decisions about my whereabouts at the time. In those days, outside of the recording studio, every element of my life was decided by a committee, with Tommy serving as chairman of the board. (Intriguingly, I was never asked to the meetings.)

As we approached town, the streets seemed to become increasingly deserted, and I began to observe a large number of police officers. Several streets surrounding the theatre were closed off and monitored by groups of guys in dark clothes, polished shoes, and black firearms. As I peered out the window at the eerily quiet streets, the vehicle slowed to a crawl. I was fighting a familiar worry that was growing inside me. I had to psychologically prepare myself to play new songs in front of new people, a performance that would be televised to millions of people on a big network. I knew I couldn't allow my anxiousness to turn into fear. Except for the cops-who had phoned all these cops? I brought my own security; in fact, I always carried security-the street behind the theatre, where the backstage door was located, was barren.

I caught a glimpse of throngs behind barricades before being rushed inside my golden dressing room. Even though I had a chance to settle in, I was still nervous. I eventually questioned why the streets were so heavily policed. What was going on in downtown Schenectady on this sweltering summer time day?

"Miss Carey," they said, "this is for you." It's because you were scheduled to appear on the show."

Apparently, throngs of youthful fans flocked to the streets in the hopes of catching a glimpse of me. I couldn't quite process this response at first. What exactly did they mean? Were the barricades, police squads, and deserted streets my fault? My first album, Mariah Carey, had been released three years previously and had hit and held the number-one slot on the Billboard 200 chart for 11 consecutive weeks, totaling 113 weeks, with four consecutive number-one singles. I had garnered nominations for Song of the Year and Record of the Year for "Vision of Love," which I performed on The Arsenio Hall Show, Good Morning America, The Tonight Show, and The Oprah Winfrey Show, and I had won Grammys for Best New Artist and Best Female Pop Vocal Performance. The album went on to sell nine million copies in the United States alone, and it was still selling all over the world (it eventually sold more than fifteen million copies). My second album, Emotions, had just come out a year prior. I especially enjoyed collaborating with David Cole (half of the fantastic C + C Music Factory). He grew up in a church and enjoyed dancing music (as demonstrated by "Make It Happen"). He encouraged me as a singer as a producer since he was one himself. For the massively famous show MTV Unplugged, I released an EP comprising live renditions of songs from my first two albums. It included a rendition of the classic Jackson Five hit "I'll Be There," which featured my friend and background singer Trey Lorenz. Following the show, the song soon rose to number one, becoming my sixth number-one hit and the second time "I'll Be There" occupied the coveted position. "Emotions" was performed at the MTV Video Music Awards and the Soul Train Music Awards. And here I was, set to take another stage, and I had no idea I was famous.

I spent four years of my life creating, performing, producing, and participating in picture shoots, video shoots, press junkets, and promotional tours. All of the prizes and honours I've earned have been presented in very organised industry settings. It just seemed like a part of the job. If I had "free" time, I spent it in an ancient farmhouse in the Hudson Valley. Tommy was in charge of everything. I was in my early twenties at the time.

I had no idea the influence my music and I were having on the outer world because I was never alone. I had no time to think or reflect. I now believe that this was done on purpose. Did Tommy know I'd be easier to manage if I didn't grasp the full extent of my power?

My then-makeup artist Billy B and hairstylist Syd Curry produced a beautiful scrapbook for me during the Music Box era, in which they gathered little notes of love and appreciation from other artists or celebrities they worked with or met on their travels. Joey Lawrence, who was such a hunk at the time (remember Joey from Blossom?), supposedly left a fairly lovely message. Tommy spotted the lovefest of a book, ripped it up, and burnt it in the fireplace before I could see it—a petty act of cruelty, especially to Billy and Syd, who went to such lengths to show me how large I was even among the stars.

I was simple to control since I had no parental or familial management or protection, but the chemistry of my connection with Tommy was complex. Tommy shielded me from my unstable family in many ways, but he went too far: he controlled and patrolled me. However, his dominance meant that throughout these early years, all of my focus, energy, and enthusiasm went into composing, producing, and singing my songs. Tommy and his grasp on my movements seemed a reasonable price to pay for the opportunity to pursue the work I had always desired. He was in charge of my life, but I was in charge of my music. It wasn't until that moment in Schenectady that I realised how popular I was. I had admirers! They would soon become another source of strength for me.

The magnitude of what I had just discovered began to hit me as I sat on a chair in the dressing room, having my hair straightened, curled, and sprayed. The cops weren't there because of some violent or dangerous situation; they were there to clear the way for me. My family may not have provided me with protection, and my relationship may not have supplied me with security, but seeing that there were so many people showing up and pouring out love for me gave me a new sense of assurance. Because Tommy never permitted me to enjoy the dazzling benefits afforded to the young, wealthy, and popular, the popularity I discovered was defined completely by my relationship with my fans and their engagement with my music. That day, I determined I was ready to devote my life to them.

I was going to debut three new songs from Music Box: "Dreamlover," "Anytime You Need a Friend," and "Hero," along with some of my known hits-"Emotions," "Make It Happen," and, of course, "Vision of Love." I had always written songs from an honest place, using my own lived experiences and dreams as a source. I also pushed my vocals to the limit. I was also planning to launch "Hero." It's always a risk to debut songs at a live event that people haven't had the chance to engage with through radio repetition. Despite the fact that I composed "Hero," it was never planned for me to perform it.

I was requested to write a piece for the film Hero, which stars Dustin Hoffman and Geena Davis. Tommy agreed that I would submit a song for the film, which would be performed by Gloria Estefan, who was signed to Epic Records (Sony, Tommy's label, was the parent corporation). I heard Luther Vandross was also working on a song for the soundtrack, so I knew I'd be in good company. I dug down in Right Track, also known as the Hit Factory-one of the major studios where I'd spent a lot of money. That day, I was with Walter Afanasieff.

In five minutes, the plot of the film was presented to everyone in the studio: a pilot goes about and rescues people. That was all I could take in. Soon after, I got up to use the restroom, one of the few things I did without being accompanied by someone on Tommy's payroll. I sat in the stall, savouring my brief period of tranquillity. I took my time walking down the corridor to the studio, savouring my time. As I went, a song and some words came to me clearly. As soon as I walked back into the room, I sat down at the piano and told Walter, "This is how it goes." I hummed the song and some of the lyrics. I began to sing, "and then a hero comes along," as Walter attempted to establish the basic chords. I walked him through what I had heard so vividly in my head.

"Hero" was written for a mainstream film and was intended to be sung by a singer with a considerably different style and range than mine. Though I thought the message and tune were very basic, I believed it fit the bill. We made a rough demo, which I thought was a little schmaltzy.

Tommy, on the other hand, saw the potential for a classic. He insisted not only that we maintain the song, but that it be included on my upcoming album. Okay, I thought. I'm delighted he enjoys it. To make the song more personal, I fine-tuned it and changed the lyrics. I went to my memory well and delved into that moment when Nana Reese advised me to hold on to my dreams. I tried my hardest to regain it, but it was a gift regardless of who received it.

"Hero" had lost its simplicity and gained some depth by the time of the Schenectady performance. My initial apprehension of singing it live for the first time in front of an audience faded as I remembered all the people who had lined the streets and packed the theatre to watch me that night. I realised that "Hero" did not belong to Gloria Estefan, a movie, Tommy, or me; it belonged to my fans, and I was going to give it to them with everything I had.

A local community organisation provided inner-city children for the Thanksgiving special. I watched the kids backstage, full of hope and dread, and I saw myself in them. I'd sing this song for them as well. The show began with my latest song, "Emotions," which was peppy and full of my typical super-high notes. I was able to really gaze at the folks in the crowd while singing "Emotions," despite the numerous stops and retakes required (singing live for TV recording is laborious work). This was Schenectady, and these were regular people, not paid extras or trendy dressed extras, but genuine, largely young people with that obvious hunger and adoration in their eyes. I saw them for who they were, and they reminded me of myself. I said a prayer and closed my eyes. As the first few notes of the piano intro played, I began to hum from the bottom of my heart. "Hero" was released into the world when I opened my mouth.

Some of us require rescue, but everyone desires to be noticed. I sang "Hero" to the people I could see from the stage. I saw tears welling up in their eyes and spirits rising. After that night, any scepticism I had about the music vanished. But Tommy had also noted the magnitude of its impact.

Later that year, on December 10, 1993, when I played "Hero" at Madison Square Garden, I declared that all domestic sales earnings would be donated to the families of those killed in the Long Island Railroad shooting three days earlier. A man pulled out a 9-mm pistol and began to fire on a train-a route I'd taken before-killing six people and injuring nineteen others. Kevin Blum, Mark McEntee, and Michael O'Connor, three heroic guys, restrained him, avoiding further murder. Because they were heroes, I dedicated "Hero" to them that night. I sang the song as part of the America: A Tribute to Heroes telethon just ten days after the September 11th attacks. And on January 20, 2009, I had the inconceivable, unparalleled distinction of performing it at the Inaugural Ball of the United States of America's first African American president. "Hero" is still one of my most popular songs. Music Box went on to be certified diamond in the United States and is one of the best-selling albums of all time.

And here's a side remark with a side eye: a handful of people have come after "Hero," as well as me, claiming royalties and plagiarism. I've been to court three times, and each time the charges have been dismissed. The first time, the poor fool who was following me had to pay a fine. Knowing how cleanly the music came to me, I initially felt victimised, but after a while, I almost learned to expect lies and lawsuits to accompany my success-from strangers as well as my own family and friends. And they're not going to stop.

That night in Schenectady, the taping took several hours. A television show requires numerous cameras, close-ups, far and cutaway shots, wardrobe changes, hair and makeup touch-ups, extras, and audience reactions-it's a production. When we finished, I thanked everyone: the youngsters, the choir, the orchestra, and the crew. Then, as quickly as I entered, I rushed out the backstage entrance, which appeared to lead not to the street but directly into the limo.

I slid into the backseat, buzzing with a dizzying mix of tiredness and euphoria. As we went out onto the street, I witnessed groups of people surging over the weak metal partitions, yelling my name and "We love you!"" I spotted the officers as well, standing there unaffected in the thick of the chaos and excitement. It was one thing to be educated, but it was quite another to witness with my own eyes, hear with my own ears, and feel in my soul how real people reacted to me and my music. What I felt that night in Schenectady was love, not idol worship. It was the kind of affection that comes from genuine connection and acknowledgment. I was transfixed as I gazed out the window, watching all these individuals lavish me with affection. Not simply followers. A household.

My high began to wear off as the crowd receded from view and we approached the outskirts of town, approaching the highway. The mood in the automobile had returned to its usual darkness by the time the wheels struck the tar of the Taconic Parkway. Tommy and I would ride up the southern stretch of this route most Thursday evenings, leaving fashionable Manhattan behind to spend the weekend in Hillsdale. As the lights and high-rises faded in the rearview mirror and the city's magnetic draw faded, so did a part of my life force.

When the car radio, which kept tuned to Hot 97 (their then-slogan: "blazing hip-hop and R&B"), began to break up, muffled by static, I knew my life as a Grammy-winning singer-songwriter twenty-something was coming to an end. Every weekend, Tommy would switch off the radio, which was my lifeline, and listen to one of his favourite Frank Sinatra CDs. Listening to Tommy croon "My Way" as he drove us back to my captivity was a heartbreaking metaphor.

On our long trip, I was trained to either speak business or be silent. But really, I just stared out the window at the majestic Hudson River, getting ready for my first important role: satisfied wife-to-be. Tommy had only ever encouraged one acting gig. Taking acting classes or accepting roles in films or on television was severely prohibited.

I don't recall Tommy and me addressing what had just transpired on the way back from Schenectady. Perhaps he realised I saw the fans' purity and power—that I'd found how their love couldn't be suppressed. It is fans, not record executives, that create a phenomenon. Tommy was astute. He was aware. But I'm not sure if he recognized that after that moment, I did as well.

When we got to the farmhouse, all I wanted to do was take a bath. Being a performer is a show. You put on and build up, plan, modify, accommodate, and shape-shift. It takes rituals (often in the form of harmful habits) to reconnect with yourself. My ritual was to clean up after the act. One of the few things I was able to make to Hillsjail was the installation of a huge tub facing a large picture window. Because installing a camera or intercom in there would have been too much for Tommy, I took refuge in the bathroom. The cool marble tile felt good on my bare feet, which had been hoisted up in heels all night. I lazily pulled off my outfit, grateful that the only sound I could hear was the water running. I turned off the overhead lights and lit a few white candles. The water was inviting, so I gave in. I dipped my head and lingered in the warm, dark silence, as if being baptised. I softly arose, tilted my head back, and propped my arms along the big basin's edge, my eyelids still closed, loving every moment of this peaceful solitude. Slowly, I opened my eyes to see a gleaming full moon against a clean, blue-black sky. I began to sing softly, "Da, da, da, da, da..."

Images of the scene I had just left flew through my head, mingling with sad memories of my brother shouting and my mother crying, of myself as a lonely little girl in a neglected frock. I was swimming in a tub bigger than my entire living space just five years ago, in a room bigger than all of the living rooms in all of the thirteen homes I grew up with my mother. The immensity, complexity, and unpredictability of the path I had taken to get into this bath struck me. It was the first time I felt comfortable enough to return to Mariah, the tiny one, and see what she had suffered. The first stanza and chorus of "Close My Eyes" instantly came to me. This song would take me years to complete-years of sorrow and survival.

My Big Fat Sony Wedding

Tommy and I brought my mother to a posh dinner in midtown Manhattan to announce our engagement. As we walked out of the restaurant, the city was decked out in its night time attire of brilliant lights and flashing billboards, and I gave her the engagement ring, a Cartier tri colour gold band with an immaculate, modest-sized diamond. It was unassuming, yet it was Cartier. My mother glanced at the exquisite, gleaming ring on my slender (and very young) finger and whispered quietly, "You deserve it." That was the end of it. She climbed into the limo I'd arranged for her and drove away. I had no idea what she meant by that. But that was all that separated us. There was no womanly advice or girlish laughter, which surprised me, but I thought the occasion called for more than a one-liner.

Many rational individuals have asked why I married Tommy. None of them, however, questioned the decision more than I did. I knew I'd lose more power as a person, and I was already emotionally drowning in the relationship. Through the music and the business, we were inextricably linked. However, our personal power dynamic was never equal. He convinced me that if we married, everything would be better, that things would be different. But what I truly hoped for was that if I gave him what he so desperately desired, this marriage that he imagined would legitimise him or quell rumours about him having an affair with an artist on the label, it would alter him. I never quite understood why he was so eager to marry. I hoped that by doing so, he would relax and release his grasp on my life. I hoped he would trust his "wife" and allow her to breathe.

I was in my early twenties, just out of the shack, and the idea of a life that comprised both personal and professional fulfilment was foreign to me. I honestly believed that I deserved neither pleasure nor success. I was used to making all of my life decisions based on survival.

I didn't choose what dazzling clothing to put on every morning back then; I chose what survival mechanism I needed to arm myself with that day. More than my own happiness, I needed my artistic career to survive. Happiness came second. Happiness was a passing fancy. I married Tommy because I believed that was the only way I could stay in that relationship. I saw the power he could give my music, and he saw the power I could give him. Our sacred union was founded on creativity and vulnerability. Tommy was a partner I admired. If only he had known how to treat me with the dignity I deserved as a human being.

I was the bride at the first genuine wedding I ever attended. When I was younger, I never saw myself getting married. I hadn't intended to. Girls fantasise about large, poofy dresses and Long Island weddings in high school, while I imagined myself as a successful singer and actress. That was all I cared about, so it was odd that I ended up wearing one of the decade's most dramatic, voluminous gowns to one of the decade's most expensive New York weddings.

Apart from the ambition, Tommy and I were diametrically opposed, and the Black half of me perplexed him. Tommy tried to wash the "urban" (translation: Black) out of me from the time he signed me. It was no different when it came to music. In their original form, the songs on my very first demo, which would become my first smash album, were far more soulful, raw, and current. Tommy smoothed down the songs for Sony in the same way he smoothed out my appearance, trying to make them more general, more "universal," more ambiguous. He always seemed to try to turn me into what he saw as a "mainstream" (white) artist. For example, dad never allowed me to wear my hair straight. I believe it appeared straightened to him rather than naturally straight. He said it made me look too "urban" (Black) or R&B, like Faith Evans. Instead, he insisted on my loose and bouncy curls, which he claimed made me look nearly Italian (albeit, strangely, my curls are a direct product of my Black DNA, aided by a nice small-barrel curling wand to incorporate the frizz).

Before I met Tommy, my curls had undoubtedly crisscrossed with Italian culture. (I did move around a lot on Long Island.) In the eleventh grade, I went to a beauty school. I was basically there to pass time before becoming a celebrity (my sole career ambition). It was more innovative, fun, and useful than traditional high school. I'd always struggled with putting together a coherent appearance because I didn't have any of the tools or potions to play with at home, and I certainly didn't have a steady group of females to go through the transition from girl to teen with. There was a tremendous attraction to honing one's beauty talents. I was also a tremendous fan of the musical film Grease as a kid, and I imagined myself having my own Pink Ladies moment. And I sort of did.

My beauty school class was largely made up of Italian girls. There were mean girls, shy girls, regular girls, and then there were the girls. They were a group of three or four gorgeous girls who, in comparison to all the other girls I'd seen on Long Island, were the most glamorous-or, rather, they seemed to be having the most fun with it. But they were so preoccupied with their appearance.

Subtlety was a waste of time and flavour for these gals. They were completely tanned. Their excessively highlighted hair was coiffed to perfection, every ringlet, puff, and bang sprayed into submission. Their makeup was vibrant, eye-catching, and flawlessly applied. They did, in fact, have lengthy fingernails. Some had nail art as well, such as a line of tiny gold studs or their initials in gems on a beautiful, thick, bright white "French"-major.

We were all required to wear a drab maroon button-up smock with white slacks and awful, hefty white nursing shoes. These girls, on the other hand, would not keep their flamboyance veiled. They wore their smocks open to show off their leggings and males' ribbed white tank shirts with elegant, lace bras underneath. And then there was the jewellery: thick and thin gold link chains in flat, herringbone, and rope patterns with Italian horns, crosses, and initial pendants dangling from them, hoops in their ears, and tiny gold and diamond rings on every finger.

They seemed very mature to me. They were plainly having sex—not only because they carried their bodies in a certain way, but also because they made it known to everyone. They chatted freely and frankly about sex (which surprised me). I had no idea what they were talking about when they dubbed themselves "Guidettes," but I thought it was interesting that they had a name, like a singing group or something.

They'd arrive at the beauty school in expensive cars, blasting WBLS, the urban dance radio station-oh, if only they knew we called it the "Black Liberation Station"-loudly. And, of course, I knew every song and would sing it, such as Jocelyn Brown's "Somebody Else's Guy" (I relished laying into the huge, slow vocals at the beginning) or Gwen Guthrie's "Ain't Nothin' Going On But the Rent." My teacher despised it since I was always singing and blowing out notes rather than doing blowouts.

Because I was from another school and hadn't acquired my own confident look-I wasn't quite cool clique material-it was my singing and frequent popping of jokes that drew these showy teen princesses over. We were able to do each other's hair. Surprisingly, no one ever questioned my mixed texture, the thickness (or thinness) of my lips, or any other aspect of my appearance. Those gals taught me a lot. They assisted me in adding volume and vigour to my hair as well as gloss to my lips.

We have more in common than one may think. In mainstream culture, there has always been an unspoken tie between hip-hop and the mob. We were particularly taken by the elegance and swagger of films such as The Godfather and Scarface. Later, for the "Heartbreaker" video, I recreated the hot tub scene with Jay-Z. That will always be one of my favourite videos. I appreciated paying respect to Michelle Pfeiffer's character, Elvira, the tortured and trapped woman with a gorgeous home and sexy luxury clothes (to which I could connect).

Despite my best efforts, I was doomed to be a beauty school dropout. The majority of the girls in my class were extremely focused and talented in their chosen subject. They were born to do hair. Fortunately, I had another lovely destiny in store for me, for I would never be crowned queen of finger waves.

I never expected that just a few years after my 500 hours with the Guidettes, I'd be standing at the altar with one of the music industry's most prominent men-an Italian, no less. I hadn't been looking for a love partner. I wasn't seeking a husband at all. And I had no intention of marrying Tommy, but it occurred anyhow. And what a spectacle it was. When I said yes to the marriage, I thought, Why not make it an event-an EXTRAVAGANZA! As with any project or production in which I am engaged, I wanted to instil as much optimism and festiveness as possible. Tommy was also excited about the possibilities for pomp and ceremony. He concentrated on assembling the most influential and impressive audience-er, guest list-he could.

There was clearly no family or mother of the bride driving the show here. This task was well beyond anything my mother could have imagined. Besides, this wedding was intended to be an entertainment-industry spectacle; even a talented mother or sister couldn't pull off the show we were planning. The post of production coordinator was assigned to the wife of one of Tommy's coworkers, a socially well-connected middle-aged woman. She assisted me with all of the key elements, like the gown.

That gown was an event in and of itself. My coordinator knew one of the most important female fashion designers of the time, who specialised in bridal gowns. I spent more time in her showroom for fittings than I did in the studio for a whole album. There were at least ten fittings-a lot for a girl who had only three shirts in rotation not long ago.

Of course, Princess Diana inspired me. Wasn't everyone? She was an inspiration! I adored that wedding, and it was truly my sole model for how a wedding should appear. I didn't grow up reading bridal magazines, and the royals definitely know how to host a wonderful wedding. In the end, that outfit contained practically every princess aspect or emblem imaginable. The crème silk fabric was so fine that it glowed. Before bursting into exaggerated poofy sleeves, the sweetheart neckline fell beautifully down the shoulder. The structural bodice was beautifully decorated with crystals and beads, erupting into a massive ball gown skirt supported by layers upon layers of crinolines. The most memorable element, however, was the dramatic twenty-seven-foot train, which required its own staff of handlers. A lengthy veil was attached to a diamond tiara. Syd Curry curled my locks to make them fall down like Rapunzel's, and Billy B handled my makeup, making me look like both a gorgeous ingenue and the Belle of the Ball. I'd come a long way since being Cinderella of the Shack. The bouquet was stunning: a waterfall of roses and orchids, sprinkled with numerous all-white flowers romantically intertwined with ivy vines. A small group of young girls pelted my feet with white petals.

Tommy also did not disappoint with his assignment-the casting was excellent. The guests ranged from Barbra Streisand to Bruce Springsteen, Billy Joel and Christie Brinkley, and even Ozzy Osbourne and Dick Clark! To top it all off, his best man was none other than Robert De Niro! My old and trusted friends Josefin and

Clarissa were among my bridesmaids, yet they provided me no comfort. Nobody could. I was terrified to death.

I barely recall the ceremony at the stately Saint Thomas Church (after all, we needed a site that could accommodate the drama of the gown).

"You and I (We Can Conquer the World)" by Stevie Wonder was our song, of course, because I chose it. At the altar, I recall my face shaking uncontrollably. But, as soon as those church doors opened onto Fifth Avenue, I heard screaming and saw swarms of people swarming every inch of pavement as far as the eye could see, camera flashes flashing like fireworks. I grinned as I proceeded down the steps. My wedding was not for all those wealthy and famous people I barely knew. It wasn't for my distant, dysfunctional family (though I do recall my grandfather, by then in the grips of dementia, lovingly yelling my name like he was on the block: "Mariah! Mariah!") It was for the fans, and we gave them the fabulous moment they deserved.

I scarcely recall the star-studded reception at the Metropolitan Club (I preferred the venue because it had "MC" monogrammed everywhere, but we didn't tell TM). I was completely fatigued. It had required a lot of effort just to prepare the event and then get through it.

I'd enjoyed a girls-only sleepover at the Mark Hotel the night before. I was obviously conflicted. My friends knew I didn't believe in the concept of marriage, and yet here I was about to put on this big show with a man who was already displaying worrisome symptoms, both professionally and personally. He would become my next of kin, and the suffocating hot mess of a relationship I was currently in with him would only worsen.

"You don't have to do this," everyone remarked. But I was convinced I had no choice. I couldn't see any way out. I was at a loss for what to do. I'd learnt how to deal with disappointment and keep going, how to make the best of a bad situation and keep working. I surely knew how to deal with anxiety. I had never known life without terror.

Tommy and I managed to pull off the wedding. We flew to Hawaii the next day. I can't call what we did a "honeymoon" in good conscience; it wasn't sweet. It wasn't romantic. At. All. We were staying at someone's place, which was already drab. I didn't care because my relationship with Tommy was never about romance, but it was officially my "honey moon-ish"...

Fortunately, the house was on the beach, and being near the ocean is always reassuring to me. I went to the toilet the next day to change into a bikini when I heard Tommy yelling on a loudspeaker. I could tell he was battling with himself. Great.

"What's the problem?"" I inquired. He was on the phone with his high-powered publicist, who was yelling and cursing because he didn't want our wedding photos on the cover of People, as we'd planned. Tommy's PR informed him that it was inappropriate for his executive image. His likeness? I mean, why go through all of that for a small corner shot, as the publicist suggested? I told him and Tommy about my thoughts. The publicist erupted.

"Are you fucking serious?!?"" He screamed at me.

Tommy did not come to my aid. So there I was, twentyish, on my honeymoon-ish, on the phone with a fiftyish-year-old man shouting and cursing at me as my fortyish husband sat there doing nothing. To top it all off, I was correct! Our wedding should have been a major cover story. That was the plan-this was show business!

I burst out crying and ran out of that house while the two irate guys yelled at each other and at me like children. I just started sprinting along the beach randomly, tears spilling down my cheeks. We hadn't even finished the wedding cake when we were back to bickering, shouting, and dismissing an outpouring me. Nothing had changed or become any better. I just ran, having no idea where I was heading. I eventually found a motel with a seashore bar. I could definitely use a drink, I reasoned.

However, when I sat down, I discovered I had left empty-handed. I didn't have a phone or a handbag, no cash, no cards, and no identification. I couldn't even find a sympathy drink to cry in. I looked like a thousand lonely young women on the beach, with my hair bunched up in a topknot and wearing nothing but a bikini and a sarong, not like a famous pop diva who had sold millions of records worldwide. I didn't appear like a newlywed on her honeymoon. If someone did recognize me, they ignored me-and no one could realise how lonely I felt.

I asked to use the phone and called my manager on collect (remember when you had to memorise essential phone numbers?). I requested that he provide the bartender my credit card information so that I could at least get a drink. I requested a frozen sweet and apologetic daiquiri. As the gravity of the situation began to seep in, I sipped it while listening to the waves breaking on the shore.

I eventually made it back down the beach to the house. But I was familiar with the procedure. After all was said and done, Tommy and I would sit in silence once more. The glimmer of optimism I'd had that marrying him might change him was swept away like footprints in the sand. That was the day I started holding my breath and resisting Tommy's undertow.

Thanksgiving is Cancelled!

T. D. Valentine was his name. Back when he thought himself a musician, it was his stage name. He liked music, and he managed to establish a lifelong relationship with it. As I previously stated, our mutual love of music, ambition, and power was inextricably linked to our personal relationship. Music was the relationship, but no matter what we tried, we couldn't make it a marriage. I truly felt in my heart that I would spend the rest of my life with Tommy. My rationality and soul, however, refused to succumb to my love, and the marriage quickly began to injure me on an emotional and spiritual level.

There was a prevalent notion that I was some smart wealth digger who scored a big-time hit maker who was now funding my princess lifestyle—that I was just sitting nicely on a throne in my thirty-million-dollar estate. The wedding undoubtedly provided the illusion, but it was only that. If there was any illusion of a fairy-tale marriage or existence, it was all fabricated. Tommy's unbreakable shelter from my family has evolved into an ironclad dungeon.

Our relationship's control and power imbalance grew. His boyhood pal was my manager. His chosen security was the strong guy he idolised in school (despite the fact that I towered over him in heels). Everyone in charge of my care had a close relationship with him. When Tommy met me, I was really young and naïve; he knew so much more about so many things, notably the music business. But I knew certain things he didn't, especially about trends and popular culture, which I suppose made him feel threatened. Anything he couldn't control seemed to frighten him.

Even the thought of me doing something he couldn't control sent him into an unreasonable frenzy. One prime, ridiculous example: in Sing Sing, there was once a copy of Entertainment Weekly on our kitchen table. It included a little essay in which a writer fantasised about a modern remake of All About Eve with Diana Ross as Margo Channing and myself as Eve Harrington—genius! Of course, I adored the original film, not just for the splendour and famous performances, but also because Marilyn Monroe played Miss Casswell, a stunning, ambitious actress, in a little but delightful role.

Tommy saw the story and became enraged—at me! He found a way to blame me for someone else's fantasy of casting me in a movie (which, for God's sake, didn't even contain a love scene!). His rage would penetrate the house and shake my entire existence, as if he were an oppressive father or warden. I got in trouble (yes, "trouble," since I felt so infantilized by him) over someone else's suggestion that I do something outside his control.

The chasm between our musical and pop cultural inclinations was wider than the chasm between our ages. Uptown Records, led by the late and iconic Andre Harrell, was the label for R&B, hip-hop, and the hybrid known as New Jack Swing in the late 1980s and early 1990s. Heavy D & the Boyz, Guy (with Teddy Riley), Jodeci, Mary J. Blige, and Father MC performed in Uptown. One of my favourite albums was by Father MC. Mary J. Blige provided background vocals and hooks for him, and he also featured Jodeci-love. I would constantly listen to them. Tommy would keep an eye on me while I was listening. He knew to pay attention to what I was interested in because he was aware of my keen ear and instincts. But I knew he wasn't feeling it. He couldn't quite appreciate its cutting-edge nature. He never truly believed in hip-hop's ongoing cultural influence because he couldn't fully comprehend it. He dismissed it as a transitory fad or trend.

Tommy and I were out with a group of friends and prominent music executives one night in a gorgeously lighted dining room in an Italian restaurant frequented by music business illuminati and serving wonderful warm focaccia. We were all seated at a large table. My Swedish friend Josefin was in town, and she and her new husband were among the attendees, so it wasn't really a work dinner, but at this point, my work, social, and personal lives were all intertwined. Even our house had been mostly intended for conducting business and impressing partners (albeit my contemporaries' major concern was where they could chill and smoke a spliff—surprisingly, we chose the studio out of all the opulent rooms offered). We'd occasionally throw large, celebratory dinners there, which were sometimes both fun and fabulous, but they never felt like family. Nothing feels like family when you are constantly watched, like I was.

I was part of a pioneering age of dynamic young musicians, songwriters, producers, and executives throughout the mid-1990s. We were determined to create a new sound based on R&B and rap but unconstrained by conventional conventions and rules. We were experimenting with new technologies and combining fluid melodies with gritty hip-hop aesthetics and energy. We were the only ones who knew how to make the music we were making sound both raw and smooth. It was our sound, reflecting our era and tastes.

My former boss was also there at the restaurant. The topic shifted to Puffy aka Sean as P. Diddy, who had recently left Uptown Records, where he had started as an intern and eventually rose to the position of head of A&R. Now he had his own record company, Bad Boy, and his star artist, Notorious B.I.G., was all over the radio and spreading across a generation. "So, what do you think of this guy, Puffy?" inquired the then-head of Epic Records. What do you suppose is the matter with him? "Do you enjoy his music?"

Because I was the youngest person at the table, he asked me the question. I also enjoyed and comprehended hip-hop, and I was the sole artist present. Besides, I'd lately worked as a producer with Puff. The table became silent as I leaned in and stated unequivocally that Puff and Bad Boy were unquestionably the future of modern music.

Tommy had recently told me and my nephew Shawn, at our dining table, that "Puffy will be shining my shoes in two years." I was taken aback. Wait. What exactly did he say? It was one of the few occasions I stood up to Tommy and told him that what he said was clearly racist. I was furious. Shawn had never seen me react angrily to him; he was taken aback by my outburst and became truly concerned for my safety. There were so many people back then.

But that night at the restaurant, what should have been a lively debate between an industry leader and an artist about global culture and the future of American pop music devolved into an enormous Tommy tantrum instead. I saw his eyes spark with familiar wrath as I finished my response. He stood up from his seat and began pacing around the restaurant, panting and puffing. He couldn't stop himself from yelling. The entire table sat in silence as we glanced at each other, unsure what the heck was wrong with him (this time) or what we should do. The entire diner observed Tommy attempting to walk himself down from a cliff that only he could see. He finally stormed back. He pounded his fist on the table, still enraged, and declared, "I just want everybody to know that THANKSGIVING IS CANCELLED!" Okay, fine.

We were arranging a wonderful Thanksgiving dinner party at Sing Sing, but he was going to cancel it because I had dared to give my honest, autonomous opinion in public to someone he admired (who had asked me what I thought). As if it were my tenth birthday celebration. The arrogance with which he announced a national holiday was cancelled was amusing even at the time. Who was going to call Frank Perdue, for example? Who was going to recall all of the Butterballs?! A clear inquiry had been posed to me. What was I meant to do, sit like a moron and not respond to the man? Everything was absurd.

What wasn't amusing was the prospect of being punished for my violation on the hour-long commute home. That night, something came over me, and I determined I wasn't going to take the blame for something that wasn't my fault. This night, I would not be confined in Tommy's Range Rover torture dungeon and returned to Bedford prison. I made the decision that I would not leave with him under any circumstances. I knew I was taking a tremendous, terrifying risk, but because we were in a public setting with a table full of witnesses, I took a chance, hoping he wouldn't create a bigger scene and I'd be safe.

He was stewing at the table, staring at me. I sat uneasily in my chair, my leg literally shaking under the white linen tablecloth, but I was still adamant. I returned the stare. Not this evening. There was no way I was going on the automobile ride with him in that condition. Everyone at the table was terrified during the tense standoff. They were terrified for me, but also for themselves. Tommy was constantly feared by everyone! But I stood my ground, and Tommy eventually walked out on his own. Even though he and I both knew there would be people monitoring me and reporting back to him, taking this position was a huge step for me. The chef and proprietor agreed to let me leave quietly through the kitchen out of respect for our privacy. Josefin and I proceeded to a little club (a huge step for me) to shake it off and have a few cocktails before retiring to a hotel for a good night's sleep. It was my first taste of independence, and I was ravenous for more.

The night Tommy "cancelled" Thanksgiving was the first time I stood up to him and defied his demands. He never let me have my own voice; even the smallest hint of agency or independent thought appeared to frighten and emasculate him. I had no say over his power. I was the label's voice, bringing in all kinds of revenues and shares for him, but I couldn't have a say at the dinner table. But I'm not going to let myself get cancelled.

The Man From Kalamazoo

Mariah's Solo Test Operation Flight Night had a rigid schedule: First, Tommy and I would dress normally and attend the Fresh Air Fund gala together, as we had done in prior years. Following that, I would eat supper with a group of pals (which is actually quite regular). I was tormented with a nasty combination of fear and ennui because going out with Tommy had become such a laborious act.

Fortunately, I knew that night that some of my colleagues, such as Wanya Morris from Boyz II Men, would be attending the event, so I wouldn't have to wear such a thick mask all night. I clung on to the fact that on the other side of the picture ops, thousand-dollar plates, and platitudes was the chance of enjoyment rather than the usual silent, oppressive trek back to Westchester together. I think I'll be able to get through this one. I stepped out on the red carpet in a beautiful red floor-length Ralph Lauren matte jersey slip dress, supported on Tommy's arm.

All of the pictures from that night showed us staring in various places, my body rigid, and an odd smile on my face. There was nothing to make me grin. To be honest, I was reluctant to grin in most images since I'd been told as a child that my nose was too big and that smiling made it wider. That jolt of uncertainty was followed by a shot of confidence from Sony's artist development executive, a rotund and imposing woman who informed me when we first met, before my debut album, "This is your flattering side." Only photograph yourself on this side of your face." (It was the side with no beauty mark. Who are these individuals? Who exactly are they?)

I was too young and lacked the confidence to oppose her, so I obeyed. Many of the harmful and vicious criticisms I received as a kid and young woman were internalised by me; some have burrowed so deeply into my brain that I will never be able to completely dig them out. Even now, when I see a camera, I unconsciously move to the "flattering side"; it's a thing.

The evening was your standard celebrity-studded charity chicken supper. I sat up straight, sucked in my stomach, and waited for it to be finished. Tommy and I acted the part flawlessly all night. We'd both got a lot of practice faking it. Then it was over: I had given Tommy his moment in the spotlight, and now I was free to go! This was a significant event! I was never permitted to go out with friends without him. It was impossible for me to believe! I was free to laugh and enjoy myself as a human being, without being shushed, silenced, or secluded. I felt like Cinderella in reverse, with the elegant ball being the chore.

Giorgio Armani was the apex of a luxury fashion house in the 1990s. Armani was the A-listers' go-to designer. Tommy, of course, donned Armani and was constantly trying to dress up. I also donned Armani on occasion. The designer employed several cool and well-connected people who hung around with their cool clients. Following the gala, we planned to attend a dinner party at a restaurant that some Armani insiders had booked. My assistant and I went, and Wanya was waiting for us. It was a fantastic downtown scene.

The lighting was dim, and we were placed in the rear against a massive wall of windows, at a long dining table piled high with gorgeous bottles of wine and candles. The atmosphere was charged with joyful banter and laughing. In the background, there was wonderful music playing, with Wanya periodically breaking out into riffs. It was a typical night for everyone else, but going out socially with my peers and listening to music from my era was a revelation for me.

I felt lighter than I had in a long time, even though I was still being observed. I felt young and free. It was not uncommon for guests to arrive and depart in waves at a dinner party of this size, so when Derek Jeter and his companion entered and sat across from me at the table, they didn't command any of my attention. They were both ambiguous in my opinion. After a brief peek up, I wondered, "Who are these guys?" My focus returned to the more fascinating dinner guests.

Even in high school, where athletes were at the top of the food chain, I was never drawn to the jock type. Derek and his companion were no exception to this norm. His Armani suit couldn't hide the Kalamazoo in him. He didn't have the polished New York vibe I'd become accustomed to. I'm not being deceptive, but he was wearing sharp shoes. Artists can be quite tribal, and when compared to the hip-hop and R&B stars, models, fashionistas, and cool youngsters of all colours at the table, the two of them appeared rather mundane.

The restaurant was sombre, but our table was humming, and the talk eventually shifted to "inconspicuous Blackness"—passing, but with more depth. I was really engrossed. We talked about who we thought was secretly Black or had some Black blood in them, how they might or might not identify, and how they were frequently misdiagnosed. I had never before had an open discussion on mixed or multiracial aesthetics. My parents didn't have the language for it, and Tommy was never interested in discussing my multiracial identity; if he wasn't ashamed of it, he certainly wasn't interested in promoting it. I couldn't believe it: it was my first night out without him, and suddenly I was having a conversation about race and identity with young, intelligent, and creative people!

The discussion eventually shifted to me. One of the Armani guys said he couldn't tell whether I was part Black (he wasn't, by the way). Wanya was having none of it. "Naw, man, come on!" he said in a loud voice. "How could you not know?" we all know. I was giggling but also quite curious.

Another member of the Armani crew joined in, "Derek, your mother's Irish and your father's Black, right?" So, what are your thoughts on all of this?"

It was like the scene in The Wizard of Oz when the screen switched from black-and-white to Technicolor all of a sudden. It was a new moment, a new room, a new night, and even a new world. When I heard "Irish mother and Black father," my head jerked up and I turned to face Derek. Our gazes were riveted. A profoundly suppressed melancholy that I had buried inside since the first terrible blow of someone telling me I wasn't white enough or Black enough, which translated into "not good enough," emerged and began to melt, and a need to connect took its place.

It was as if I suddenly saw him. Derek was no longer a commoner; he was more akin to a Prince Charming. This first moment of bonding was quite powerful. I had written an infinite amount of romantic moments in my songs, and I had been quite depressed for a long time. Finally, I felt as if I were in a dream. I saw his eyes, which were big flashing jade pearls floating in a golden-brown pool. There seemed to be no one else in the restaurant or the world. We started talking across the table, and our conversation was bright, dazzling, and extremely flirty. I couldn't remember the last time I'd felt butterflies while talking to a man, if there had ever been one.

We talked softly and casually throughout the rest of the evening. I eventually understood that everyone was aware of our desire, but I didn't care. This was my night out, and I was enjoying the freedom, the adrenaline, and the allure of it all. I was aware that I was being observed, but who cares? Derek, like myself, was young, multiracial, ambitious, and working at his ideal profession! We felt like the only ones in the world in the midst of all the people, lights, and music. It was still on fire, even if it was only a flicker.

Despite my bravado, I let Derek lead me to the car, where a driver-aka Tommy's agent, of course-was waiting. Being with him seemed like life at the time. I'll never forget walking alongside him that night, looking up at his height and the way his muscular physique moved. I felt small next to him. It was a whole different experience. This two-minute journey down the street seemed more thrilling than walking a thousand artificial red carpets. It was an unforgettable experience. The humid late-night breeze blew my hair and pressed the delicate jersey of my dress against my body as I strolled through the streets of New York. I was actually feeling fantastic. Unencumbered.

The Last Show at Sing Sing

With the rain on the roof, a dormant seed of self had been watered, and some of Tommy's dampness had lifted. I had developed just enough self-assurance to appear belligerent. Look, I—we—knew we were at the end of the road before I went. Tommy began making desperate last-minute attempts to get me to stay as I began to leave in increments. He gave me a beautiful but useless Carnival red convertible Jaguar with a crème leather interior and matching drop top. It lay in the driveway of our thirty-million-dollar estate, adding to the opulent scrap heap that was our marriage.

One evening, I was working with two men with whom I had a significant creative and professional relationship, and whose role it was to show Tommy mobile loyalty. These three guys, to whose riches and stature I had made significant contributions, and I were sitting in the kitchen, prepared to eat. Despite the fact that we were all "friends" sitting around the table in front of a large, rustic fireplace with the now-sadly ironic phrase "Storybook Manor" etched in the limestone mantel (I named it that, desperately believing I could wish and will my nightmare into a fairy tale), the atmosphere was anything but warm. It was frigid, quiet, and scented with grief and struggle, proof that something in me had changed. I believe Tommy was embarrassed that he had lost control and had lost his "woman" in front of his "boys." He was furious by his embarrassment.

He launched into an embarrassing and unsettling rant about the wonderful automobile he had just given me, our fabulous estate (which I planned and partially funded), and how, despite all of this, I wanted to leave him. Tommy stepped over and picked up the butter knife from the place setting in front of me while I sat motionless, looking down at the table. He pushed it against my right cheek on the flat side.

My face squeezed every muscle. My entire body stiffened; my lungs tightened. Tommy was holding the knife there. His boys stood there silently watching. He dragged the thin, cool strip of metal down my scorching face for what felt like an eternity. I was enraged from the humiliation of his terrible, cowardly behaviour in my kitchen in front of my "colleagues."

That was his final performance at Sing Sing with me as the captive audience.

I was trapped in the bathroom, which had turned into a mausoleum, sitting on the edge of the frigid tub, trying to summon the confidence to leave totally. "Don't be afraid to fly," the words quietly flutter into my head. Extend your wings. "Please open the door." I hummed the melody that would later be known as "Fly Away (Butterfly Reprise)." And for the last time, I descended the majestic stairway. I genuinely believed I would die in the house I built in Bedford and be haunted by it for the rest of my life. I could only imagine it as a morbid yet joyous tourist attraction, "The Famous Ghost of Mariah Mansion," similar to a classy Graceland, where you could hear me belting high notes in the halls at night.

When I ultimately left Sing Sing with only my outfit and personal photos, the only thing I really desired from the house was the gorgeous hand-carved mantelpiece. A superb Eastern European craftsman had carved it to my exact design specifications. As I was departing, I stroked my fingers along the house's smooth and delicate curves as a final farewell. Only then did I spot a butterfly in the centre of the heart in the centre of the building. I didn't ask for it, but its open wings were the indication I needed when I let the door close behind me.

Natural calamities eventually tore down all of the barriers that had kept so much of my anguish within. Sing Sing burned to the ground a few years after I departed. A tornado also entirely devastated Hills Jail. I was in my Manhattan penthouse when I got a call from the former owner of my former house. She had removed the mantel but stored it since it was so special to her and she felt I would desire it. I got it back and had it refinished in white lacquer, just like Marilyn did with her mother's piano. That mantel is currently in my most personal room, along with my family portraits and other sentimental items. And I didn't let go of my spirit.

PART III: ALL THAT GLITTERS

Firecracker

The Glitter story was a convergence of terrible luck, bad timing, and sabotage.

The album and film were originally titled All That Glitters, and while I began working on the project in 1997, we had to put it on hold for several years to allow me to meet more essential duties at Columbia. While I had much creative control over the soundtrack, I had almost none over the film. The early story concepts I produced were almost entirely altered. I began writing the script with my acting coach and Kate Lanier, the author of What's Love Got to Do with It? She's a fantastic writer, and I had complete faith in her. But we started getting more and more studio notes every day.

Tommy couldn't give up control, especially now that I was doing what I'd always wanted to do but feared: acting. Glitter was produced by Columbia Pictures, which was owned by Sony, and was linked to Tommy. While we were working, the chair of Columbia Pictures referred to him as "the white elephant in the room"-that silent, invisible power we couldn't talk about. Anything that would have pushed the threshold, making it an R-rated or even PG-13 film, was quickly nixed. Nothing could be more genuine, edgy, seductive, or down-to-earth. There was a much grittier screenplay available (come on, it was the 1980s!), but we ended up with something pretty bubblegum.

We had script changes every day as a result of the constant back-and-forth and Tommy's suffocating control. Nobody knew what was going on at any one time. In addition to a drastically different storyline, I had envisioned Terrence Howard in the lead (this was before Hustle and Flow, mind you). But the powers that be were contemptuous of the concept of Terrence and myself having a romance. I figured it was because he appears darker than me (though he, too, is mixed!) and they had no idea how it would work, if you catch my meaning. So that was a letdown. No disrespect to Max Beesley, who was fantastic.

Aside from a lack of creative freedom, I thought my acting was seriously hampered for a variety of reasons by the acting teacher, who, by this point, I believe had gotten overly invested in my profession. I don't want to kill her, but she kept me from doing my best by putting her own trash onto the film. This is something I've heard happens a lot in collaborations; it got very Marilyn and Paula Strasberg-ish. With all due respect, it devolved into an ego trip (I'm sure she'd agree with me now). What was crucial to me was that the extras and other individuals on set—from performers to crew—knew I was serious, eager to learn, and willing to work as hard as they did. Though the overall experience was not ideal, I believe I delivered several strong performances (which would have been more apparent with better editing). I wasn't unhappy because it was such a new medium for me, but I believe there were mistakes at every stage.

But there was a glimmer of hope at the end of this glittering tunnel. Dani Janssen was once described by Frank Sinatra as one of Hollywood's "original broads," and I adore a good broad, especially one who knows how to throw a nice party. Dani Diamonds' (as she was dubbed) Oscar celebrations are legendary—and I don't use the L word lightly. To be invited, most visitors must either hold an Oscar or have been nominated for one. Her regulars include Sidney Poitier, John Travolta, Quincy Jones, Oprah, Babs (Barbra Streisand), and many more legends. Every year, a fresh new crop of Oscar winners mingle with icons among her vast collection of white orchids. I was lucky to receive a surprising and very special invitation one year (naturally, Dani and I hit it off famously). "I know people give you shit about it," commented one of the hottest leading males at the time, a two-time Academy Award winner (Dani's code of no "networking" or name-dropping is taken very literally, so he shall stay unknown). I've been there before. You were hitting some extremely authentic notes, and I believe you should keep doing so. Don't let them convince you that you can't go there anymore." He made me feel so much better because I have so much respect for him as an actor. And it's a good thing I didn't give up since something genuinely "precious" would come my way a few years later.

Tommy was at the root of most of what went wrong with Glitter. He was enraged by my divorce and departure from Sony, and he used all of his influence and connections to punish me. And everyone else, including my new label, was aware of what was going on. Tommy and his pals even went so far as to steal promotional items from record stores, such as my stand-up advertising. It was a true battle. He didn't want it to appear like I could succeed without him, so he even messed with the Glitter soundtrack. I worked on it for a long time with folks like Eric Benét and Brat, both of whom were in the film. Terry Lewis was able to obtain the original music for "I Didn't Mean to Turn You On," of course, because he and Jimmy Jam produced it! And having Rick James on "All My Life" (who required a white suit, a white limo, and possibly some other white accoutrements for his session) was priceless.

The whole thing felt like a dream. And in many respects, it was exactly what I had hoped for for so long. Don't get me wrong: I'm not suggesting Glitter was Cat on a Hot Tin Roof, but I don't believe it deserved what it got. I believe it could have been good if it had been allowed to be carried out as initially planned, but by the end, it was such a battle just to have it happen at all. But, as always, I remained optimistic. Everything will work out, I told myself. I went to that hopeful place. This is difficult right now, I assured myself, but I'll get through it no matter what. And on the other hand, I was stronger than before. And, despite the fact that darkness followed, it was in that darkness that I learnt to create my own light.

Tommy was enraged when I severed the cords he was using to control me. He would never allow me to be a tremendous success after leaving him and Sony. He wasn't going to let me or Glitter shine; instead, he was determined to get us. He wouldn't have been happy unless I completely failed. He was fond of saying, "You do what you do, and then I do my magic." He'd have me destroyed before I revealed that he wasn't a magician. If the Glitter soundtrack had been a smash hit, he would have had to admit that he was not almighty, that he was not indispensable, and that he did not create Mariah Carey on his own. To add to his rage, he knew I'd just secured the biggest cash record deal in history (as did my family, but more on that later). On top of that, I was creating a movie, which he had forbidden when we were together, which meant my career was expanding, which made him feel like he was contracting. He'd already been publicly humiliated when I left him, so how could I succeed without him? That was too much for his weak ego to bear. What does it mean for his entire kingdom to be built on fear? What would it mean to other artists if I completed the project without him? I was convinced he was committed to me not having a life outside of his control. That he wouldn't be satisfied until I was buried.

I escaped a man and marriage that nearly killed me. I was one of numerous artists that chastised Tommy and his cronies for acting against the best interests of the organisation for petty personal vendettas.

Meanwhile, at the new label, chaos reigned since "Loverboy," the first single from the Glitter soundtrack, was only at number two on the charts, rather than number one. I didn't understand the uproar about a number two single from a soundtrack for a film that hadn't yet been released. But, suffice it to say, after filming Glitter, my life and profession were once again subjected to intense scrutiny and pressure.

There was also sabotage. I'd written the words to "Loverboy"; the melody was tight, and the beat was addictive. Clark Kent, the film's super producer, and I had chosen "Firecracker" by Yellow Magic Orchestra as the sample, and the few insiders working on the production were in love with it. Sony execs (and spies) took note of this. I had chosen the song and paid for it to be featured in the film. Sony raced to develop a single for another female entertainer on their label (whom I don't know) after hearing my new song, which used the identical sample I used. They utilised the sample from "Firecracker" and released it before "Loverboy." Tommy was ringing up his management Irv Gotti, begging him and Ja to cooperate on a duet for the same female entertainer's record-leaving me scrambling to rework the tune. Irv even mentioned it on Desus & Mero: "He knows we just did this shit with Mariah... and he's trying to fuck with Mariah." Simply put, this was sabotage.

Look, I was well-versed in the art of converting shitsituations into fertilizer, but Tommy knew fucking with my creative choices was especially low. But I wasn't going to let him stop me. I changed gears and went from the techno influence to a funkier sample from Cameo's "Candy" (you can't go wrong with Cameo), then Clark Kent produced it once more. He saved the day after we were both robbed with a pounding tune (using some fragments from "Firecracker," which is my favourite section of the song). Da Brat said it all in her blazing and honest verse on the remix to "Loverboy."

Larry Blackmon (with cornrows) was even featured in a poppy sexy-kitschy video filmed by my dear friend, the fabulous David LaChapelle. Despite everything, we had a nice time.

But things were about to get a lot worse.

Calamity and Dog Hair

My mother hadn't returned from the city with the record-label delegation at the hotel, which reassured me. It meant I wouldn't be triggered by her and Morgan together, and I didn't want to waste the little energy I had left trying to explain to her why I just needed to sleep. Fortunately, I had my girl Tots as a buffer. As we got closer to the house, I started to feel a little better. This is the house I bought for my mother and family to live in, to find comfort in. Now I was the one who needed it the most. I'd planned a guest bedroom for anyone in the family who needed a place to stay, which I knew I'd need now. In my mind, I could already picture its inviting warmth. All I wanted to do was get some food in my stomach, go upstairs, close the door, and fall asleep before my mother arrived home.

I was straining to hide how wrecked I was as we stepped inside the house, especially in front of my nephew Mike, who was still living there. He was only a child, but he had already gone through a lot with his addicted mother. I wanted to spare him the painful past that was coursing through me and all of us. But I was also starting to panic as I realised I was now cut off from the city and my true house. I didn't have a driver, I was with Morgan, and my mother was on her way back. They could be toxic and manipulative when combined. I could feel myself swinging back and forth between the house and the shack. I was now in their world. The past and the present both felt unsafe.

The place smelled like disaster and dog hair. I scanned the chaos and clutter. (I never liked the way my mother kept the house; that's why I always had cleaning workers for her.) I've always liked things to be very clean, much like my father. For me, a mess brings anxiety. I started putting things in order, which is something I do frequently to refresh myself. I reasoned that if I could bring some order to the turmoil in the house, even in a minor way, I'd be able to stay in my body. But I continued falling.

I told myself that I wasn't helpless. This was the lovely home I had purchased, built, and managed as an adult. I wasn't a tiny girl living in a ramshackle shack. I can put some order to this mess. But I was exhausted. Maybe, I reasoned, we were back in the shack due to a time and space anomaly. I needed to rest. Desperately. And I was hungry. My thoughts began to race once more.

I went to the kitchen to see if I could find something to eat. When I visited my mother, I would usually bring all of the necessary supplies, including disposable plates and cutlery, to ensure that everyone had enough to eat and that the cleanup was simple. The sink in the kitchen was stacked high with dirty dishes. I knew that focusing on a simple activity would help to ground me. Washing the dishes would suffice. I'm going to do it. I'm going to do the dishes, I reasoned. I'm going to eat till my plate is empty, then I'm going to bed.

I immediately remembered as I reached for the faucet. It's been six days. I haven't gotten more than two hours of sleep in six days. My hands shook as I attempted to accomplish the work I'd set for myself. I could only hear my heart pounding inside my chest. What exactly am I doing? I'm doing the dishes. Right. After what seemed like an age, I finished one plate and hung it on the rack. I then reached for a sudsy dish, but it slipped through my fingers and clattered to the floor. I tried again, and this time I succeeded. I fumbled one. I was now responsible for cleaning up the dish and water on the floor. The noises of running water, banging plates, and people conversing mingled. I was hurriedly trying to tidy things up and get out of the house before my mother arrived. When I bent down to pick up the dish off the floor, the light dimmed and the sounds faded. The space surrounding me began to close in on me, and I began to drift away. I went black for a split second but was able to recover before collapsing totally.

I did it. The anxiety spikes were gone, but so was every ounce of my energy and willpower. But, if I couldn't sleep normally, passing out would suffice. I walked up the stairs toward the guest room with Tots' aid, picking up clumps of dog hair on the way (I was barely conscious, but my standards were still alive). I was a tired refugee, and I felt I had discovered exactly what I was looking for. I gave in to the softness of the bed and slumped upon it. Everything immediately changed to the long-awaited darkness, and I sank into it. Finally, there is serenity.

"Mariah! What exactly are you doing? They're on the lookout for you!" A loud, dramatic voice yanked me from the depth of silence in which I had been floating. I was jerked back into consciousness, lost and sputtering, to see my mother looming over me. My mother had jolted me up from my first slumber in nearly a week! To make matters worse, she was waking me up to tell me that the record label was seeking for me to get me back to work, as if she were some kind of agent for the machine that had consistently prioritised my earning potential over my well-being.

That was the breaking point. I did, in fact, leave my body. Something deep within me came fast up and out of my throat, savage and raging.

"Well, I gave it my all!" 'I tried my hardest!"You never say anything else!'" I yelled at her in her exaggerated tones. It was a justification I'd heard from her countless times throughout my life. I'd finally gotten to sleep in the house I'd bought after six days of being pursued—six days of hiding, fear, and near death; six days of no rest; six days of trauma—only to be awoken by my own mother. My mother, who had found solace in that house I had worked so hard for!

I wasn't anticipating a hug or a kiss on the cheek, nor was I expecting homemade chicken soup or baked cookies. I hadn't anticipated a warm bath. I had not anticipated a massage, steaming tea, or a goodnight tale. I wasn't anticipating any comforts from a healthy mother for a sick child. I knew my mother wasn't capable of that kind of parental response; after all, I was the one in charge. I looked after her and everything else. I wasn't expecting her to make me feel better, but I certainly wasn't expecting her to wake me up! My wrath seized control. I couldn't see, hear, or feel anything in my body.

As a survival reflex, I went into the depths of my sarcasm and ruthlessly mocked her. When faced with intense stress or trauma, I developed a defence mechanism of cutting to humour.

"Well, I gave it my all!" I tried my hardest!" I mockingly imitated her over and over. I was trying to wake her up to the harsh absurdity of the situation using her own words. I knew it was bad, but every filter I could have used to stop myself had been removed.

"I JUST WANT TO GO TO SLEEEEEP!" I screamed."With each word I hurled at her, all my fears, all my resentment, all the years of impressions I'd done of her behind her back—all my anger was thrashing out."

"Well! I! Did! The! Best! I! Could!" I yelled.

No one had ever seen me in such a wrath, especially not my mother. Morgan and Alison were always the ones who would burst out laughing throughout my childhood. They would scream and yell at each other while throwing condiment bottles at each other. They were going to fight. They would scream and threaten my mother, or they would knock her out cold. My brother and father got into a fight. But now it was my turn to let it all hang out. I wasn't being violent or throwing obscenities, but I was still having a good time.

I was in a rage, hysterical fit, but I couldn't stop thinking about my nephew Mike. I didn't want to repeat the sickness cycle that we'd all been through. I was standing in front of his door, sandwiching my mother, my rant, and his innocence. I'd asked Tots to look after Mike before we arrived; I trusted her because of the innumerable nieces and nephews she'd cared for over the years. I never knew what could happen to my family, so she was soothing him behind the closed door. "This has to stop!" I screamed. We must break the cycle!"

All of the rage and fear I had stored up inside me was now directed at my mother. She was at the heart of the cycle I was determined to disrupt. My mother was finally witnessing the full extent of my rage and was ill-equipped to comprehend or de-escalate it. She didn't get the joke-in fact, she felt threatened and ashamed by it. She shook her head, then an iciness enveloped her, and she threw me a look that screamed, Oh really? You dare to make fun of me? You're going to threaten me? You have no notion who you're up to.

When my mother is terrified, she activates her total faith in the historical proof that whiteness will always be protected—and she frequently phones the cops. She'd called the cops on my brother, sister, and even my sister's children at various occasions. Even when she didn't feel threatened, my mother contacted the cops. I took my family to Aspen for Christmas one year. It was the first year after I left Sing Sing that I was determined to start my own ultimate Christmas tradition, so I invited the entire Carey family. Christmas signifies family to me. I rented a house so I could decorate and cook home-cooked meals for my family, and we could sing Christmas songs at the top of our lungs if we wanted to, and I put my family up in a fantastic hotel.

We were all hanging out at the house at one point when Morgan became outrageously intoxicated. When he went missing for a while, my mother resorted to her typical dramatics.

"What happened to Morgan?"" she screamed. "I can't seem to find Morgan!"" Morgan was a thirty-something grown man, but my mother was still in a self-induced panic." "I can't seem to find Morgan!"" She contacted his hotel room several times but received no response. So, what exactly did she do? She contacted the police. My mother summoned the cops in Aspen, Colorado, to locate my nonwhite, occasionally drug-dealing, been-in-the-system, drunk-ass brother. The cops arrived at the motel, and everything went downhill from there. She requested that they smash down his hotel door, behind which Morgan was found naked, butt up, and passed out on the bed. The news travelled like wildfire around the area, and Morgan and Cop Caller Mom were never invited to spend Christmas with me in Aspen again. I'm not expecting much for Christmas. Especially not the cops.

As a result, that night in Westchester, she also phoned the cops on me.

As is customary in white, affluent communities, the police arrived soon. My mother pushed open the door. "Is there a problem, ma'am?" an officer inquired."

"Yes, we have a problem," she said, letting the two white cops into the house. I could tell they recognized me, even though I was still in a bad mood and looked at it. For the first time in nearly a week, I had passed out and fallen asleep. I had swiftly put my hair into a bun in a chaotic emotional whirlwind. I was dressed in leggings and a T-shirt (like one might when trying to sleep at home). I had gathered myself somewhat, because that's what you do when the cops are involved. But I wasn't wearing my superstar mask, which is how practically everyone recognizes me (except, of course, the Lambs). Without all the glitz and dazzle, I appeared unsettled, even a touch wild or ill.

Though the officers were technically in my home, their focus was on my mother. She gave them a strange, knowing glance that felt like a secret-society handshake, some sort of white-woman-in-distress cop code. She'd been defied, and I'd dared to be aggressive. I was being hostile toward her. I was frightened of her. They heard her signal loud and clear. It was part of their training. Her culture has a code.

Her world, her people, and her language were all here. She was in command. Even Mariah Carey couldn't compete with an anonymous white woman in trouble. I would have woken up ready to make a DVD if I had just been allowed a day or two to relax. Instead, I was standing in front of my mother's (really, my) house with the cops.

The most alarming aspect was that I was too tired to detect my source. My light was blocked by the evil energy of my mother, Morgan, and the cops—the entire situation. Tots was someone I needed to see. She, too, had a tremendous God in her life, and if I couldn't access mine, I hoped I might sense hers. I thought she could keep me safe in a sisterly, spiritual way. I was trying to be strong for her, but she was also terrified of the cops. And who could blame her? It's very understandable. She was the only person in the home who was clearly 100 % Black. How could she explain to her mother that she'd been detained in an upscale neighbourhood and was in some upstate jail after successfully avoiding police for years in the Brownsville projects? Lord knows what they would have done to her in there (this was before #BlackLivesMatter and cell-phone activism, and even a movement hasn't stopped the majority of the cruelty). Tots was doing her best to keep herself and Mike out of the way of the chaos. Tots knew she was out-privileged and completely out-powered against two white cops and one white woman in upper Westchester.

Morgan was hiding out in the little den we called the "Irish room" because of his lengthy, violent history with law enforcement. No one tried to explain to the cops that it was simply a family blowout—that everything was fine, and I was just exhausted and had lost my temper. I needed help, not cops. But no one stood up for me. The cops only observed a terrified white woman in a large house full of nonwhite people.

I let go, betrayed, humiliated, and overwhelmed by reliving the neglect and anguish of my youth. I didn't have any fight left in me, but I knew better than to fight the cops. I was finished. I was relieved, ironically, that the cops could take me away from this place of trauma and betrayal. My brother had enticed me back into the dysfunctional world that he, my sister, and my mother had inhabited when I was a child. My mother had kidnapped me in my sleep and then handed me over to the authorities. There was nothing else for it but to capitulate. I consented to have the police remove me from my own home in exchange for one basic request: that I be allowed to put on my shoes. My family could take my pride, trust, and the last of my vitality, but they couldn't take my dignity.

I put on some heels (perhaps mules), neatened my ponytail, slapped on some lip gloss, and climbed into the backseat of the cop car. Being pulled away by cops was obviously unpleasant, but I was defeated and needed to flee by whatever means possible. The car's comfortable seat cushions and ballistic armour created a warped sense of security. My body reminded me that it was still in desperate need of rest. Morgan slid into the seat behind me.

I looked at him, empty, unwilling to understand what my family had just done to me. It was impossible for me to believe. I had to delegate my anguish in order to pin it on someone else. I reflected on how it all started-when did everything start to go apart?

In a fog, I said, "This is all Tommy Mottola's fault."

Morgan's eyes sharpened, and he smiled sinisterly once more. He nodded, "That's right." "That's right."

We drove off into the night.

Snow globe of joy

I was standing on a stunning, cheerfully decorated stage, dressed in a bedazzling red sequined gown inspired by Marilyn Monroe's attire in the "Two Little Girls from Little Rock" act in Gentlemen Prefer Blondes, during my sold-out 2019 Christmas show in Madison Square Garden. My face was lit up not only by the excitement of the event, but also by the talented hands of my stunning long term makeup artist, kiki-confident and great friend Kristofer Buckle. Tanaka was on one side, with Roc and Roe in their own little joyful ensembles (they did a special performance of "Rudolph the Red-Nosed Reindeer " that night!). Behind me were my "singing siblings"-my brother, Trey, and sisters Tots and Tekka, who have been with me through all of my seasons, difficult and peaceful. And there were tens of thousands of my magnificent, diverse, vast family of loving fans in front of me.

When I peered out, I saw wonderful flocks of Lambs dressed in sequined onesies and other glittery attire (the arena was awash with sequins, studs, and crystals!), waving signs and holding hands. There were little girls in crushed-velvet dresses on their fathers' big shoulders; old men with no hair next to young women in headwraps; gay, straight, fluid, trans, nonbinary, people who were liberal, conservative, devout, agnostic, abled and disabled; people of every shape, hue, persuasion, and belief you could imagine.

And as I gazed upon the marvellous multitudes, I saw Liron, a woman who was once a twelve-year-old girl who had the lyrics to "Looking In" written on the door of her Tel Aviv bedroom, now a woman who is an invaluable member of my inner team and a treasured, loyal friend. I saw the knowing eyes of girlfriends and colleagues-people I'd worked with, laughed with, and grieved with throughout my life. My global family of followers, who have provided me with unrivalled, unstoppable, and unconditional support since Day One, were spread out in front of me like a crystal-clear ocean of love.

For years, I wished I could gather five people to sing in unison at

Christmas, and now I'm in a family of thousands of Lambs, supporters, and friends, and everyone is singing "All I Want for Christmas Is You" together! They were singing to me as well as with me. Our voices were booming so loudly and joyfully that the entire city of New York could have heard us and joined in. We were all connected in our own universe of Christmas spirit at that moment. Tons of white confetti flakes fell from the ceiling on top of us. It seemed as if the entire universe had joined me in one enormous snow globe of delight!

The next day, I awoke fatigued but ecstatic to see the Billboard headline: "Wish Come True: Mariah Carey's 'All I Want for Christmas Is You' Hits No. 1 on Hot 100." After a 25-Year Wait." What?!

I received my twentieth number one at the end of 2019! The Lambs did it yet again! My fans made it the most streamed song in the world in a single day! I had worked hard and focused with my little team to give the song a lot of energy on its brilliant silver anniversary, but reaching number one is huge! That can only be done by true fans, not marketing strategies.

After the joyful frenzy of "All I Want for Christmas Is You" ended, I made my annual pilgrimage to Aspen, my own winter utopia. I was ready to cuddle in with my blood and chosen family-Roc and Roe, Tanaka, Shawn and his wife, and two of my dogs, Cha Cha and Mutley—and let our new customary festivities begin! The days were clear and fresh. The grassy fields beyond our homey-yet-sprawling chalet were buried in thick crystal-white snow, as if sparkling clouds had landed in our backyard to slumber. Instead of staying in our toasty onesies all day, the kids and I layered on our big coats and ski boots and ran out into the fluffy blanket of flakes to make snow angels. We let the fresh smell of pine wash over our faces and tickle our nostrils as we gazed up at the beautiful blue sky.

The joyful bustle of the family warmed the entire house. From Handel's Messiah to the Jackson 5, Christmas music provided an endless soundtrack (complete with laughter, dogs barking, and children running in the background). The halls, the walls, everything was decked out and decorated, and the fireplaces were roaring. The large tree in the living room was decorated with white lights, gold balls, cherubs, and gilded butterflies, and was capped with a magnificent angel star with gold-tipped wings and cream gossamer fabric flowing down from them. (There is always another old-school-style tree with large, multicoloured lights in the family room, giving a fuller, much happier Charlie Brown vibe. We decorate it with homemade decorations and cheerful Polaroid images of one other; I also include treasured ornaments donated to me by Lambs from all around the world throughout the years.) White candles and poinsettias surrounded garlands and lights cascading down mantels and doorways. Cups were filled with delicious butterscotch Schnapps and luscious hot cocoa.

My favourite Christmas foods are my father's linguine with white clam sauce (on Christmas Eve, of course) and stuffed shells. Santa stops here to spread some holiday cheer, and we ride and sing on a two-horse open sleigh, eh! We sing Christmas carols and play in the snow. It is true. It's quite loud. It's entertaining. It's called Joy. It is my universe.

During our Aspen retreat, I was already feeling grateful (and full of hot chocolate and Schnapps) when another Billboard headline broke: "Mariah Carey Becomes First Artist to Reach No. 1 on Billboard Hot 100 in Four Decades, Thanks to 'All I Want for Christmas.'" Yes, thank you to the fans who adored my little Christmas love song so much that it remained at the top of the charts for three weeks, making it the final number-one song of 2019 and the first number-one song of 2020, the first year of a new decade... What exactly is a decade?

After all of the swirling, toasting, singing, and revelry. People dispersed to find a spot to sleep for the night. Everyone else was content in their bedrooms, while the kids were curled up in the family room watching a movie. I crept into the living room and sat by the fireplace. Except for the stars glittering outside the wide windows against the black-blue sky and the warm amber glow from the fire, everything was dark. I relished a beautiful, peaceful, personal moment with myself. I took everything in.

I am at ease.

I am finished.

Printed in Dunstable, United Kingdom